# More Praise for *Be the Boss Everyone Wants to Work For*

"Using a unique combination of research, straight talk, and humor, Gentry brings to light all of the barriers that keep new leaders from succeeding (including the ones we don't talk about) and offers clear-cut, actionable strategies to face those barriers head-on to become 'the boss everyone wants to work for.' It's clear that Gentry has a deep understanding of what it takes to develop strong leaders. This book has become required reading in my organization."
—Brené Brown, PhD, LMSW, author of the *New York Times* #1 bestsellers *Daring Greatly* and *Rising Strong*

"At last, a research-based yet exceptionally hands-on book focused on one of the toughest boundaries to span—the one from superstar individual to manager. Gentry has captured the direction leadership development needs to go—sustainable, action oriented, and a total departure from old ways of thinking."
—Chris Ernst, Global Head, Learning, Leadership, and Organization Development, Bill & Melinda Gates Foundation, and author of *Boundary Spanning Leadership*

"Basing his work on both social science and practical experience, Gentry provides usable tools to help people become 'the boss everyone wants to work for.'"
—Jeffrey Pfeffer, Thomas D. Dee II Professor of Organizational Behavior, Graduate School of Business, Stanford University, and author of *Leadership BS*

"In a humorous and compassionate voice, William Gentry offers practical, helpful advice to new leaders about what they must do to flip their way of thinking and acting to become the kind of boss people admire and want to support with their best efforts."
—Stew Friedman, Practice Professor of Management, The Wharton School, and author of the bestsellers *Leading the Life You Want* and *Total Leadership*

"Every leader makes mistakes, but new leaders won't make nearly as many if they follow Gentry's advice. I wish a book like this, which explores the foundations of leadership in a highly engaging style, had been available early in my career!"
—Ingar Skaug, retired President and Group CEO, Wilh. Wilhelmsen ASA

"For smart, practical guidance on becoming a boss, there's no better authority than William Gentry. His insights are grounded in first-rate research and the realities of organizational life—and refined by his own experiences as an up-and-coming leader."
—**John R. Ryan, President and CEO, Center for Creative Leadership**

"Get this inspiring book into the hands of all your new leaders—it will accelerate their growth and build the leadership bench for your entire organization."
—**Vice Admiral Cutler Dawson, US Navy (Ret.), President and CEO, Navy Federal Credit Union**

"This book is a must-read for first-time leaders, or those aspiring to be leaders. It also serves as an invaluable reference for human resource professionals to develop their next generation of leaders."
—**Marcia J. Avedon, PhD, Senior Vice President, Human Resources, Communications and Corporate Affairs, Ingersoll Rand, plc**

"William's research-based insights, heartfelt personal examples, and simple framework for practical application ensure this book will become beloved by new managers and the folks who develop them alike."
—**Alison Smith, MSPOD, Vice President of Organizational Design and Development, Caribou Coffee and Einstein Noah Restaurant Group**

"Drawing on both his own personal experience and a wealth of empirical research, William Gentry outlines how new leaders must 'flip their script' to succeed in their new role."
—**Kevin Kelloway, Canada Research Chair, Saint Mary's University**

"William Gentry has provided an easily digestible framework for new managers that is backed by deep-dive research. There's no arguing with this book—it's thoughtful and data driven from beginning to end."
—**Tasha Eurich, Principal, The Eurich Group, and *New York Times* bestselling author of *Bankable Leadership***

"It's about time! Finally a down-to-earth, compassionate, actionable book for every new supervisor who has wondered, 'What have I gotten myself into?'"
—**Elaine Biech, author of *New Supervisor Training*, ATD Workshop Series**

"Fortunately, it's never too late to make the six life-changing flips that William Gentry describes in this profoundly insightful book."
—**Joe Tye, CEO and Head Coach, Values Coach Inc., and author of *All Hands on Deck***

BE THE
BOSS
EVERYONE
WANTS TO
WORK FOR

# A GUIDE FOR
# NEW LEADERS

William Gentry, PhD

Center for
Creative
Leadership®

BK

Berrett–Koehler Publishers, Inc.
a BK Business book

**Berrett-Koehler Publishers, Inc.**
1333 Broadway, Suite 1000
Oakland, CA 94612-1921
Tel: (510) 817-2277    Fax: (510) 817-2278    www.bkconnection.com

**Ordering Information**
**Quantity sales.** Special discounts are available on quantity purchases by corporations, associations, and others. For details, contact the "Special Sales Department" at the Berrett-Koehler address above.

**Individual sales.** Berrett-Koehler publications are available through most bookstores. They can also be ordered directly from Berrett-Koehler: Tel: (800) 929-2929; Fax: (802) 864-7626; www.bkconnection.com

**Orders for college textbook/course adoption use.** Please contact Berrett-Koehler: Tel: (800) 929-2929; Fax: (802) 864-7626.

**Orders by U.S. trade bookstores and wholesalers.** Please contact Ingram Publisher Services, Tel: (800) 509-4887; Fax: (800) 838-1149; E-mail: customer.service@ ingrampublisherservices.com; or visit www.ingrampublisherservices.com/Ordering for details about electronic ordering.

Berrett-Koehler and the BK logo are registered trademarks of Berrett-Koehler Publishers, Inc.

Printed in the United States of America

Berrett-Koehler books are printed on long-lasting acid-free paper. When it is available, we choose paper that has been manufactured by environmentally responsible processes. These may include using trees grown in sustainable forests, incorporating recycled paper, minimizing chlorine in bleaching, or recycling the energy produced at the paper mill.

Library of Congress Cataloging-in-Publication Data

Names: Gentry, William A., author.
Title: Be the boss everyone wants to work for : a guide for new leaders /
    by William Gentry, Ph.D.
Description: Oakland, CA : Berrett-Koehler Publishers ; Published with the
    Center for Creative Leadership, 2016. | Includes bibliographical references and index.
Identifiers: LCCN 2016014040 | ISBN 9781626566255 (pbk. : alk. paper)
Subjects: LCSH: Leadership. | Executive ability. | Management.
Classification: LCC HD57.7 .G4574 2016 | DDC 658.4/092—dc23 LC record
available at https://lccn.loc.gov/2016014040

First Edition
21   20   19   18   17          10   9   8   7   6   5   4

Book producer: Westchester Publishing Services
Cover designer: Ian Koviak / The Book Designers

*This book is dedicated to the 297 new leaders who were part of my research, the literally millions of entry-level and first-level supervisors, managers, and directors on the frontlines, and everyone who is, or is about to be, a new leader. You can be the boss everyone wants to work for.*

# Contents

# Introduction

*The Biggest First in Your Professional Career*

Firsts. There are many "firsts" in our lives. First date. First kiss. First concert. First car. First album or CD (or MP3) you bought and listened to. First time leaving home. First time "with" someone, if you catch my meaning. First heartbreak. First child's birth. Think about these "firsts." I bet you remember a lot about those or other important "firsts" in your life.

Here's another "first"—your promotion into your first managerial role, the first formal leadership position you've ever had. All you've known in your career is work, work, work. And you were crushing it. The reward? You're a boss for the first time in your life.

Think about your own story. Do you remember when you heard the news and found out that for the first time in your life that you'd be leading others? How did it make you feel? Did you feel like this new leader, an engineer by trade?

*Throughout your early years of employment, you always questioned leadership. You continually asked questions like*

1

*"Why can't we do it this way?" or "What are they think-*
*ing?" or "Is it really that hard to just do it?" When you*
*become a leader, you'll quickly realize why these questions*
*aren't easy and why things were done a certain way. You'll*
*be in charge of employees, which is a great thing. But you*
*also have to answer to a different group, a group with*
*"grown-up" agendas, whose members know this business*
*inside and out. They may question whether they made the*
*right choice in promoting you. This group, which now*
*includes you, will lead the future of the company, and its*
*members have certain processes that need to be followed or*
*things don't happen. These processes are usually the answer*
*to why things are done a certain way, and as an individual*
*contributor you just didn't know all that was going on.*

*With all this said . . . I'm the youngest of a new*
*generation of leaders. Deep down, I know there is room*
*for improvement, that some processes could use a change.*
*Change happens for a reason, and I'm not afraid to be that*
*reason.*

Or maybe this new leader's story is more like yours:

*I was sitting in my vice president's office. It was a Friday. I*
*gave "the business case" for the raise I felt I deserved. Stating*
*how indispensable I was, how my skills were unique, and*
*presenting the evidence supporting the impact I made on*
*our department and the bottom line, it all worked like I*
*planned. Finally, I was going to get that raise I had been*
*asking for all this time. I never felt so vindicated. Then it*
*comes:*

*"You know, one of the key areas of focus for the*
*executive team in our organization is developing top*

*talent. We've always thought that you'd be a great
manager. You and I have talked about this before in
passing, and you always said, 'Now's just not the right
time.' But I really think that with this raise comes
more responsibility. Isn't it time that you step up into a
leadership role in our department?"*

*"Interesting," I said.*

*"We think you're ready," my vice president said.
"It's a once-in-a-lifetime opportunity. Our department
needs you, and our organization needs you. So, can
you do it? We can sign the paper today, and we can
make this official on Monday."*

*"Wow. This is huge. I'm flattered. It's definitely
worth considering. But I have a question. I've never
managed anyone before. Do you just expect that
Friday I am a regular employee and Monday, magically, I'm a manager?"*

I'm sure your story is unique, meaningful, and memorable
to you. This person sounds sort of reluctant, realizing the mag-
nitude of this "first" in his life. But maybe you're like most
people, excited to jump right in and do it, like the engineer.

Having that supervisor, manager, or director title, or
something similar, looks good on your business card, doesn't
it? You should feel proud—it's a big deal. And as a new leader,
you probably hope to be a great boss, a boss everyone wants
to work for.

But what does that even look like?

Well, there are the "bigwigs" and "top dogs" of business,
military, politics, religion, or sports you've admired. You might
aspire to be them one day, so those are good examples. Or
you've been lucky enough to have a great boss; that's a good

place to start. Of course, many of us suffered under horrible bosses (not too unlike the movie), so that tells us what we shouldn't do.

You have your own ideas on how to be a great boss. Don't you want to know how those ideas hold up to the facts?

## Don't Believe the Hype

Let me set the record straight, and make this very, very clear. The boss everyone wants to work for is not a perfect, energetic, popular, animated, outgoing, gregarious, touchy-feely, audience-rousing, maverick of a rock-star celebrity who is the smartest in the room, everybody's friend, and is not just liked, but beloved by all. We might aspire to this, but think about it. The best bosses you worked for weren't all of those things, were they? Of course not. So, don't put that type of pressure on yourself.

They also aren't the all-knowing, godlike, self-admiring, self-involved, brownnosing, micromanaging, big-headed, rude, controlling, scream-at-and-threaten-people-to-get-the-work-done loners and jerks who talk a good game and say all the right things, with a win-at-all-costs attitude to boot. That's not the answer either.

The science I'll present and the stories you'll read describe how you can be the type of boss everyone wants to work for. It is possible. But with that may come different reactions. No doubt, you're eager to get on the fast track, and what a great way to start. Maybe you feel joy and acceptance, like you finally made it. Maybe you're scared. Yeah, you could feel some dread. The thought of you getting stuck with it may cross your mind too. But in the end, you know you deserved it. You think you can master being a leader just as quickly as you mastered the work that got you promoted into leadership in the first place. The opportunity to change so many things at your organization for the better is there. And like any "first," you know as well as I do that you will never get a second chance at leading others for the first time in your life. You don't want to blow it. The pressure is on. Bring it.

Regardless of how you felt or under what circumstance you were promoted, I am willing to bet this: no matter what profession, function, or field you are in—working behind a desk, on the sales floor, or out in the field; working for the government, a not-for-profit, a Fortune 500 or otherwise; woman or man; young or old; in the United States, United Kingdom, Saudi Arabia, Singapore, or any place in between—the reason behind your "I-just-got-promoted-into-management-for-the-first-time" story and experience is shared with almost every other new leader out there:

> *I was an individual contributor or professional who got promoted into my first managerial role because I am highly competent; I have a track record of exceeding expectations; I am damn good at what I do; and, much like a superhero in a movie, I have a very special set of skills that make me who I am.*

So maybe you have a particular set of skills. But as an industrial-organizational psychologist who studies and conducts research on effective as well as failed leaders, and as someone who designs and trains leadership development and executive education programs specifically for new leaders, one thing I've come to know is this:

*Exceeding expectations and having a very special set of technical skills helps a person stand out from others and makes a high-performing employee, and possibly a kick-ass movie hero. It does not necessarily make a boss everyone wants to work for.*

## The Price of Being an Ineffective New Leader

It's funny that you were probably promoted into your first managerial role and became a boss due to your individual success, technical savvy, subject matter expertise, and smarts. Funny because all that and a Starbucks gift card will only get you a venti iced skinny hazelnut macchiato, extra shot, light ice, no whip, when it comes to leading others. Ironically, as a new leader, you can't rely on most of the things that got you that promotion into leadership in the first place. New leaders must do something much more substantial and, frankly, much more different from anything they've ever done before in their professional careers. It's probably why so many are struggling, even failing, in their new gigs as bosses. Each of us could probably talk about one right now or, worse, feel that way about ourselves. And the numbers would back these stories too. Consider the following findings over the past decade:

- Eighty-two percent of frontline leaders (where many new leaders are in organizations) are *not rated as "excellent"* in skills and capabilities as leaders.[1]
- Eighty percent of frontline leaders are *dissatisfied with the job they are doing as leaders,* and 70 percent of their senior managers agree.[2]

- Forty percent of newly promoted leaders *fail* within the first 18 months.[3]
- Fifty percent of managers are labeled as *incompetent*, a *disappointment*, a *wrong hire*, or a *complete failure* by their coworkers.[4]

Organizations are promoting those who have never led before into important leadership roles at entry- and first-level positions on the frontlines mostly due to their great technical skill, their subject matter expertise, and excellent performance. And the numbers say what many of us know firsthand: *New leaders on the frontlines are struggling, and it's hurting the people around them, their productivity, and their engagement.* Poor frontline leadership is the reason engagement programs are ineffective, and employees feel unhappy, uninspired, and less empowered.[5] Upward of 60 percent report a loss of engagement, productivity, and turnover when there is poor frontline leadership, and in fact, one out of four organizations report a loss of profit due to poor or ineffective frontline leaders.[6]

## The Raw Deal of Becoming a New Leader

These stats and stories hide an important fact: New leaders get a raw deal. Actually, many of them get no deal at all. If you're a new leader reading this, odds are you probably know—and feel—what I'm talking about. According to a recent CareerBuilder survey,[7] almost 60 percent of new leaders receive *nothing* in formal training or development when they become a boss for the first time. Nothing. Just a "We can make this official on Monday" congratulations and an expectation that as soon as HR approves the promotion, they will lead others just as effectively, if not better, than middle-to-senior-level executives who have had years of leadership experience. Or as one new leader told me when he became a boss for the first time:

> *I got a congratulatory handshake from my manager and this piece of advice as he walked away: "Now don't screw it up." That was the training and development I got as a new leader.*

Can you think of any occupation or job, any task or skill, any time when people take on something new that they've never done before and receive no training, no counseling, no orientation, or no prep work? With the added expectation that they excel right from the start? Would you put someone behind the wheel of a car, big rig, motorcycle, or airplane without months of proper training? There are orientation programs for new employees. There's marriage counseling for "nearly wed" couples. There's Lamaze class for expecting parents. In almost everything that you do, where something is about to happen that is "new" and unique and that you've never done before, or some part of your life is about to change, there is almost always something new to learn and some sort of support in place to help you understand what's going to happen to maximize your success.

And it's not that way for those of us new to leadership? Ridiculous.

Becoming a leader for the first time in your life is no doubt one of the biggest psychological and emotional shifts you will ever experience in your career. It's totally different from what you do in your normal, everyday work as an individual contributor. It's inconceivable that you aren't getting any training, development, or help, given your importance. You are part of the biggest population of leaders in organizations: entry- and first-level managers, supervisors, or directors on the frontlines. You are often regarded as the most important leaders to the long-term future of organizations. You directly supervise and lead more people than any other managerial level in organizations.[8] You often have the biggest impact on team productivity, employee engagement, and customer satisfaction.[9]

Yet so often nothing is done to help individual contributors transition into leadership when they've never led anyone before. And those fortunate few who actually do get help get way less in time and support than a mid-to-senior-level executive, who usually gets two to five times more development dollars than a new leader on the frontlines.[10]

And what's even more troubling? The pressure to make this transition quickly. I frequently ask people, "How many days does it take for you to finally conclude that a person promoted into his or her first managerial role failed in making the transition?" When I average responses, the answer comes out to a little over 20 weeks (143.8 days to be exact).

Ridiculous. And sadly, true.

You and other new leaders are getting a raw deal, as if you were being set up for failure before you even get started. That's why my passion is helping new leaders like you successfully transition into becoming the boss everyone wants to work for.

## Why This Book?

I want to help new leaders by turning the research I conduct and know into practical, actionable content you can use now in your leadership role. Whether you are on the fast track and about to be a boss for the first time; you just got promoted into leadership for the first time; or you've only been a boss for a few months, this book is for you. It is designed for the almost 60 percent of new leaders who get nothing when they become a boss for the first time, and to help others who received some training and development, but by no means the time, help, resources, and attention deserved.

But let's say you've had that supervisor, manager, or director title on your business card or LinkedIn profile for a while now. You've been a boss, but it's gotten old. Maybe you're one of those statistics; you never received the training and development to enhance your knowledge, skills, and abilities when you got promoted long ago. Even though I just said you never get a second chance to lead others for the first time, well, this is your golden ticket. This book can help you by giving you what you may have never received.

If you want to be more than that title on your business card and you want to step up your game, there's hope. This is your fresh start. You can be a new leader and the boss everyone wants to work for.

As you read this, there's probably some eye rolling. Hey, I get the potential hypocrisy in all of this. Writing about how to be the boss everyone wants to work for is so much different (and easier) from actually *being* that boss. It would be like someone who has never been a parent writing a book on parenting and expecting people to buy it, read it, recommend it, and for it to become a best seller. Anybody can write a book on leadership these days. Just include what people like to hear, sprinkle in some feel-good inspirational stories, anecdotes, testimonials, and advice, right? You don't even have to be a leader to write such a book.

Although that could work, would you be willing to risk your success as a new leader on unproven opinion and advice that rarely has credible evidence to back it up? By those who may have never lived a day being a boss or can't even remember what it was like being a new leader?

I get how you feel, because I would feel the same. I'd be curious, hesitant, skeptical—maybe even a little cynical and critical. I get it because I am it: As I wrote this book, I got promoted into my first managerial role ever, as a director. One day I was a researcher, and I still consider myself to be a damn good one. But now I'm a new leader. In fact, that reluctant leader you read about earlier? That's me. Here's the rest of that story:

*"Wow. This is huge. I'm flattered. It's definitely worth considering. But I have a question. I've never managed anyone before. Do you just expect that Friday I am a regular employee and Monday, magically, I'm a manager? . . . Plus, I'm writing a book for new leaders. If I take this director position, I won't have time to write the book, which means a lot to me. Being a boss takes up so much time. I train them and I've heard their horror stories. I know I've said it before, but I still feel the same: Now's just not the right time."*

*"Well, don't you think it's the perfect time since you've done the research on what it takes to be a new leader?" My VP continued, "You can use your research to help yourself as a new leader. And your experience, along with the research and training you do, can help so many new leaders out there who'll read the book. That's a win–win for everyone."*

I'm not saying I was "guilted" into taking the position. But my VP used my own research and passion to help new leaders and those who deserved to get help but never did when they stepped up into leadership, to persuade me to take the position. And it worked. That's why I think this book, more than any other out there right now, is so uniquely positioned to help you and other new leaders. I use research, best practices, my experience training new leaders, and stories from the frontlines (including my own) to persuade, educate, move, challenge, and inspire you as a new leader your first time out, or this time around, to be the boss everyone wants to work for. I want this book to help you transition from acting as a successful individual contributor and technical expert to thinking and behaving like a leader.

So how is this book any different from the thousands of other books on leadership? Because it delivers the triple threat: science, practice, and art. I research new leaders. I train them. I *am* one of them.

## The Science: I Research Them

I'm a quant-geeky researcher—I admit it. I'm an industrial-organizational psychologist, and proud of it. I love research and have a passion for using it to help convince leaders what to do (and not do). Particularly new leaders. The scientific research I provide in this book is either tested over time or is the newest and best out there. In fact, my latest research examines almost 300 new leaders for the sole purpose of this book. What you'll read is customized to help new leaders and those on the frontlines. So, if you need reasons why you should do things to be the boss everyone wants to work for, they're not based on my opinion. It's the science and research that will tell you why.

But I promise, you won't find a bunch of statistics, equations, and correlations here (I know that's a relief; no offense taken). What you will find are insights separating fact from fiction, from my knowing and doing the research and all the reading and writing of academic articles, blogs, and tweets that come with it. You will clearly understand what the research means for new leaders and what to grab from it.

## The Practice: I Train Them

I've had opportunities to train other, more seasoned leaders. But I have a place in my heart for new leaders and managers working on the frontlines. They are so important to the success of organizations and impact the lives of so many people. And as I said, it's ridiculous that they don't get the help and support they deserve.

From my experience designing and training programs specifically for new and frontline leaders, I feature these best practices, based on good science. In this book, you have the best knowledge at your fingertips and the answers to many questions new leaders often have. Some will be quick and easy fixes; others are more difficult and will take time. All are applicable to you, and can be used in the moment, or as part of long-term developmental plans to help you succeed.

## The Art: I Am Them

Science explains why. Practice says what. But one of the best ways I've found to understand and help you and other new leaders be effective is the how. *How* do you do this "leadership thing" anyway? *How* do you apply the science and the practice? The only way is to speak from the successes, mistakes, and experience of actually being a leader. That's the how. That's the art. And it is all detailed in this book.

Unlike most new leaders, I knew exactly what I was getting into, based on my research and from the hundreds of new leaders I've trained. That's why I was so hesitant. I knew it would be difficult before I even started. Being a boss for the first time in your life is not as glamorous as everyone thinks. At times, it's thankless.

I totally sympathize and empathize with every single new leader out there. I've felt and experienced what you'll likely go through or what you've already faced. You can't rely on the technical skills that got you promoted. Dealing with people more than you had to (or wanted to) before may be demanding. Letting go of the work that you loved doing can leave you confused, frustrated, or threatened. It's awkward and uncomfortable at times. You get angry. You sometimes feel alone and lost. Doubt starts to creep in. You start second-guessing yourself. There are times you don't feel very bright—maybe even feel like you're on the verge of total failure. You feel no one really "gets" you and your situation.

But I do. I've felt all those things.

But there's the flip side as well. As a new leader, you can make a difference in the lives of others and your organization. You help people set, meet, and even exceed their goals and expectations. You can inspire others to greatness. That sense of a "win" when your team helps others, develops the next big innovative product, or lands that whale of a client is exhilarating. I know how valuable you can be to the people you lead and serve.

As a boss promoted into his first leadership position ever, I'm right there with you, and that's one of the main reasons why I wanted to write this book. I wanted to help all new leaders out there get it right this time, with stories backed by sound, reliable evidence and advice that is tried and tested. But whatever you do or however you feel—frustrated, worried, apprehensive, afraid, overwhelmed, or worse, thinking that "I can't do this"—I truly believe you can be the boss everyone wants to work for. There is a way. Just follow this one main idea in everything you do as a leader: Flip your script.

## chapter 1

# Flip Your Script So You Won't Flop as a Boss

This book provides one overarching theme for new leaders to be the boss everyone wants to work for: *Flip your script.* I believe you can truly be the boss everyone wants to work for if you are willing to flip your script.

First, let's be clear on what a script is. Think about a play, musical, movie, or television show you've watched. It was scripted. It used written text to guide the performance. And you know those scripts; you can spot them a mile away in romantic comedies, Shakespearean plays, Greek tragedies, thrillers, or dramas. You could probably write the script about these people: the third wheel; the bridesmaid who is never the bride; the party-like-a-rock-star, wicked-funny, good-looking hero; the devious villain; the jock; the nerd who gets the girl in the end; the wallflower who was beautiful all along. These people do what they are supposed to do, act the way they are supposed to act, and live the way they are expected to because of the scripts that are written for them by writers.

But scripts aren't just for jocks, nerds, villains, heroes, and heroines on stage and screen. We all have scripts in our lives.

In your own life, you write your own script and live your life based on what your script says about the various roles you have: parent, child, partner, spouse, sibling, community activist.

Your script helps you understand who you are and how to live. It's what is expected of you. When you write your own script, you provide details about how you are supposed to think; what you are supposed to do; how you should act, feel, relate with others; how you should view the world; and how you should view yourself. Scripts help us understand our roles and our purpose.

## The Individual Contributor Script and a Breakup Line

At work, you definitely live by a script. Oddly enough, the script of a successful individual contributor reminds me a lot of that old breakup line many of us have used—or, like me, heard all too often—when someone's about to get dumped. You know the one: "It's not you; it's me."

So what does that breakup line have to do with the script of an individual contributor, you may ask? Well, have you ever noticed where the spotlight and center of attention is when someone uses that "It's not you; it's me" breakup line?

Not you. Me.

No doubt, many successful individual contributors and technical experts shine the spotlight, not on "you," but on "me, myself, and I" to get success. The script usually goes something like this:

*Keep my head down. Work harder than everyone else. Push to get things accomplished. Rely on my technical skill, knowledge, resourcefulness, and unparalleled effort to get ahead. Do my job and do it well. That's how I will separate myself from everyone else and become a subject matter expert and well respected at work. That's how I get rewards and recognition. That's how I will get ahead.*

The script is the reason individual contributors get promoted into their first managerial role:

*I got promoted to my first managerial role because of my dedication, my drive, my initiative, my work ethic, my technical skills, and the accomplishments I made that directly contributed to the success of the team and organization.*

It's all about "me, myself, and I" as an individual contributor. That "me" mentality is at the heart of the script of individual contributors, technical experts, and professionals everywhere. And we've been living this script ever since we can remember, even as kids, to get ahead, to get attention, to outshine everyone. Focusing on "me" and "my" talents, knowledge, efforts, and unique set of skills and abilities brought awards, accolades, recognition, and approval. It made us successful in our educational endeavors and in extracurricular activities. And at work, that's how we became valuable and successful individual contributors, subject matter experts, and well-known professionals in our organization, if not more broadly.

The script works, and there's nothing wrong with it for individual contributors and technical experts. And because the script worked for us before, we think it should work as new leaders. Why wouldn't it? Like the saying goes, "If it ain't broke, don't fix it."

But here's the problem. Many times in life, the situation changes, and we neglect to alter our scripts to be successful in that new situation. So we keep living that same script each and every day, not knowing that it just doesn't work. That's why I think many new leaders stumble from the start. What so many new leaders have come to know (oftentimes too late to do anything about it) is that success in that new boss role is no longer defined by "It's not you; it's me."

Yes, the script for an individual contributor ain't broke. But it won't work for a new leader. The script of a boss that everyone wants to work for is different.

## So What Must You Do? Flip Your Script

The script for individual contributors is all about "me" and "my" own abilities, achievements, technical expertise, and personal desire to get ahead. That's not necessarily a bad thing; having ambition and seeking personal excellence are worthy traits. It's perfectly normal for us to be motivated to succeed and do well in life. It's the reason individual contributors were promoted into leadership in the first place.

But to be a successful leader, to transition from a technical expert to a leader of people, you must be willing to shed the "individual contributor" role that got you the promotion to leadership in the first place and stop shining the spotlight on "me, myself, and I." You must want to change, truly believe that you can change, and be 100 percent committed to change. Actually, strike the word *change*—*flip* is a better word than *change*. You must want to *flip*, truly believe that you can *flip*, and be 100 percent committed to *flip your script*. I believe you can truly be the boss everyone wants to work for, if you are willing to do this.

So what does "flip your script" mean?

Well, you know the script of an individual contributor. It's like that old breakup line: "It's not you; it's me."

To be the boss everyone wants to work for, flip it:

*"It's not about me anymore."*

Flip your script from "me" to "we." Flip from a "me mentality" to putting attention on "we" and "us."

It sounds so simple, doesn't it? Maybe too simple. But you know as well as I do, it's so difficult to do. Just look around. So many of us see (and work with) leaders who haven't flipped their scripts, like this one:

> *Lee, sales are down 15 percent this month. You know I pride myself on being at the top. I always was when I was in your shoes, not too long ago. So buckle down. Work harder. Call more people. In fact, that sales lead call you have in ten minutes? I'll sit in, and you introduce me to Ms. Oakes—that's her name, right? And then I'll take over and show you how it's done. I had to do the same thing with Vicki earlier today too. Do I need to remind you of all the incentives we'll get if we meet the targets I set? I am not going to have my meeting with Mr. Scott and tell him I missed our group's goal the very first quarter I took over sales.*

That old script—that relentless determination to complete work, reliance on technical savvy, being a subject matter expert, that focus on "me," to get rewards, recognition, and impress others—is nowhere in the script of a new leader who wants to be the boss everyone wants to work for.

So what would it look like if that new leader flipped his script? Maybe something like this:

*Lee, I've noticed sales are down 15 percent this month in the reports. What's your opinion on why? . . . Hmmmm, I didn't know there was a process issue. And it's affecting others on our team too? So what do you think could be done? . . . Lee, that's a great idea. Can you write a memo detailing your thoughts, clearly showing how your idea can better our sales? I'll be sure to tell Mr. Scott and mention that you came up with this great idea. And that call with Ms. Oakes in ten minutes—is there anything I can help you with? No? Well, I know you've got this, I have confidence in you. Afterward, let's have a 15-minute debrief and talk about the call, what went well, and what you learned from that call that will help you in future calls, okay?*

That's the type of boss everyone wants to work for, a boss who flipped his script.

Clearly, the situation has changed now that you are the boss. As a new leader, your script is much different from the script of an individual contributor, the script that you've lived your entire life, the script that made you successful and got you the leadership position. It's no longer about being better than others, about what "I" can do, "my" technical savvy, abilities, expertise, knowledge, and ability to get all the work done, proving "my" worth. Realize that the biggest driver of any new leader's success is not about "me" anymore. Make others—your staff, your team, the people you lead and serve—successful and help them fulfill their potential.

This is your wake-up call to stop living the "It's not you; it's me," script. Flip your script from "me" to "we," and embrace

"It's not about me anymore." Flip from being the center of attention to shining the spotlight on others.

## Six Ways to Flip Your Script

Flipping your script is a huge idea, a big deal. It goes against every normal and natural instinct you may have. It's so different from everything that has made you successful up to this point in your career. But leading others is so different from anything you've ever done before.

It's difficult to do. So don't take it for granted. The chapters of this book will help you with six parts of the script you must flip in order to be the boss everyone wants to work for.

### Chapter 2: Flip Your Mindset

You'll realize how to avoid derailing at such an early point in your career (and later in life too). Based on my latest research of almost 300 new leaders, this chapter will help you flip your mindset to start thinking like a new leader.

### Chapter 3: Flip Your Skill Set

Individual contributors rely on their technical skill to do their job and get ahead. That's their script. But many new leaders struggle because (1) they rely too much on technical skills that a boss clearly does not need, or (2) they were never told what skills they needed to be successful leaders in the first place. Through my latest research, I've identified four skills that new leaders often struggle with the most. So flip your skill set. You'll read about *communication* and *influence* in this chapter. *Leading teams* and *developing others* come in the next two chapters.

## Chapter 4: Flip Your Relationships

As a new leader, your relationships are different. For instance, your former peers—some possibly being your friends—now report directly to you. Plus, you actually lead a staff or a team of people. In this chapter, you'll understand the relationship aspects of leading others.

## Chapter 5: Flip Your "Do-It-All" Attitude

To be the boss everyone wants to work for, it's not about doing all the work anymore. As a boss, you'll flip your script in the way you define, think about, and conduct work, which includes developing others.

## Chapter 6: Flip Your Perspective

Individual contributors usually have a narrow view of the organization. As a new leader, flip your perspective and expand your view. Here, you'll understand what "politics" really is. Plus, you'll gain the awareness and ability to navigate the politics inherent in your organization through your political savvy, including "managing up" and working in a matrix.

## Chapter 7: Flip Your Focus

New leaders must understand that their actions and decisions can have repercussions far beyond themselves. So, flip your

focus. You'll appreciate the importance of integrity, character, doing the "right" thing, and building trust, now and as
you climb up the organizational ladder.

## Chapter 8: Stick with Your Flipped Script

Finally, Chapter 8 will help you stick with your flipped script
to be the boss everyone wants to work for.

That's a lot to take in, I admit. If you think about it, there
are entire books on the topics each chapter presents. To make
it manageable and easier for you to flip your script, I'll provide a couple big takeaways in each chapter. You can put that
information to work immediately, and you'll have opportunities to continue your learning (along with some exclusive
content, more tips, and several other answers to the old "Just
tell me what I have to do" appeals) in "The Coach's Corner"
at the end of each chapter and on the companion website
(www.WilliamGentryLeads.com).

And know this: you don't have to take on flipping your
entire script all at once. Like one of my mentors says, "You
don't have to try and swallow the entire ocean." After reading the book, you'll know the one or two areas you can start
to flip (and "The Coach's Corner" and companion website will
help out a lot too). You can be the boss everyone wants to work
for, and this book will show you how. Flip your script.

## The Fine Print. Or "This Book Isn't for You If . . ."

With all that being said, here's "the fine print" that you must
read. Here are four not-so-subtle points you should consider
before reading the rest of the book. Warning: Myths will be

shattered. If any of these describe you, return the book and get your money back.

## Point 1. If You Believe Leaders Are Born, Not Made, This Book Isn't for You

It's an easy cop-out: "I wasn't born a leader, so I'll never be a leader." That excuse is no longer acceptable. And it wasn't even true to begin with. No matter who told you or what you've heard, being born into leadership is not necessary to be the boss everyone wants to work for. Science actually debunks that old adage "Leaders are born, not made"—it's total garbage, or at least 67 percent garbage. The scientific study of genes and leadership[1] exposes that, at the most, one-third of leadership is born. That means two-thirds is made. Even my own research at the Center for Creative Leadership (CCL) uncovered that a majority of top leaders of organizations around the world think leaders are more made (i.e., can be developed) than they are born.[2] (This is just one example of how I am going to use science and research to help you flip your script and be the boss everyone wants to work for. See? That wasn't so bad.)

And if science isn't enough, just look around your own organization or consider the people you know in the world. Granted, most of us will never be president, admiral, general, superintendent, or CEO. No matter if these positions are on your radar or not, you don't need to have credentials the length of your arm, come from privilege, or have the necessary "genes" to be the boss everyone wants to work for. So many of us are underdogs who can rise up through the ranks, without privilege, money, or fame, and become great leaders. You shouldn't feel leadership is impossible, that you'll never be able to get this "leadership thing" because you're not famous, not a one-percenter, or not at the top of your class. You shouldn't feel that because you aren't a born leader, you'll never have the chance to be one. And if people are telling you that, buy another copy of this book and show them, or use it to hit them over the head with it (okay, bullying probably isn't the answer, as you'll read in Chapter 2). So, first, if you firmly believe that leaders are born, not made, this book isn't for you.

### Point 2. If You Expect That Transitioning into Leadership Will Be Easy, This Book Isn't for You

If there were some magical "if X, then Y" flowchart that worked 100 percent of the time, or if there were an app that guaranteed success in each and every situation you encounter as a new leader, I would give it to you. But when you lead others, easy fixes are rare and more likely than not, difficult. However, it can be rewarding. So, second, recognize that it is hard to flip your script. It will take effort but will be so worth it in the end. However, if you think you'll breeze right through with no sweat, this book isn't for you.

### Point 3. If You Are Afraid to Make Mistakes, This Book Isn't for You

It's a cliché and it's true: We all make mistakes. We all have things we should work on. When you flip your script, allow yourself to make mistakes. Be vulnerable. Research professor Brené Brown studies and speaks about the importance of being vulnerable and how it can help you lead an authentic life (check out her powerful 2010 TEDx Houston talk on You-Tube[3] and her various books, such as *Daring Greatly*[4]). Here's one story of a new leader being vulnerable, admitting faults, weaknesses, and imperfections:

> *I remember an assessment that my coworkers took to rate me in terms of how effective I was in different areas of leadership. Yeah, I gave myself some 3s, just to keep my ego in check. But mostly 4s and 5s. Then I got the data from my coworkers. At first I was surprised. Then I became angry. Then I was very hurt. I felt like a total failure. Getting a 1 or a 2 on "communication," or "delegating," or "resolving conflict" is not enjoyable to see, particularly when I thought I was doing rather well in those areas, especially communication—it's a major portion of my research! How can I be horrible at something that I study and write so much about?*

That new leader is me. Clearly, I'm not perfect at leading others. Neither was the engineer I mentioned earlier. The nearly 300 new leaders in my research who are the foundation of this book, or others you'll read about, are not perfect. Neither is your boss. Even the most successful leaders who have made it to the top of organizations or their fields were not perfect. You don't need to be either.

Though you'll read a lot of success stories, many times you learn even more from your mistakes, weaknesses, hardships, vulnerabilities, and even failures. Our research over decades at CCL says hardships and failures help make leaders who they are today.[5] I will be sharing the challenges, weaknesses, mistakes, and failures of new leaders I have studied and trained, and my own shortcomings, failures, and lessons learned. Let these stories help you navigate being a new leader or help you rectify any recent mistakes you've made as a boss.

All of us make mistakes. We oftentimes fail. But the best leaders learn from them. And in fact, those mistakes and failures some may see as a strength, as in this comment about one of the best performing new leaders in my study:

> *One of his strengths? He admits his own failures and weaknesses. That lets his team know it's okay to do the same.*

Perfection is not a prerequisite to be the boss everyone wants to work for. Allow yourself to be less than perfect. Allow yourself to make mistakes and learn from them. Allow yourself to be vulnerable; it may actually help you. But if you can't, this book isn't for you.

## Point 4. If You Don't Want to Flip Your Script, This Book Isn't for You

Finally, it's like I tell all the new leaders I train:

> *I can't guarantee you will succeed. But those who are successful—they wanted it. They believed they could flip their script. You can come to CCL or any other prestigious place in the world to get leadership development, to get the best training money can buy. But if you are unwilling to flip your script, if you don't see the point, all the training in the world will not work. Just like the research shows, you have to want to flip your script and believe you can do it.*

Well-known theories on motivation, self-efficacy, goal setting, and control, as well as tons of research, all reiterate that if you want to flip your script, you can. But you must be willing to shed the "individual contributor" role that got you the promotion to leadership in the first place. You must value flipping your script, clearly see how flipping your script will positively affect outcomes important to you, see yourself able to do it, and have support from others.

The glue that holds this book together, every single research-based tip, tool, and piece of advice I provide in this book and elsewhere, all of it is based on one single thought: *flip your script.*

So, anytime you are in a situation and wonder, "What should I do?" ask yourself:

> *Have I flipped my script? Am I looking out for "me" and putting "me" in front of everyone else? Or have I truly flipped my script and realize, "It's not about me anymore?" Is it truly less about "me" and more about "we" now? Is more time being invested on getting things "I" want, or on helping others—my direct reports, staff, team, coworkers— develop and grow and getting something we all want?*

More times than not, you won't go wrong being the boss everyone wants to work for if you flip your script. Leaders are great when they want others to succeed, when they realize, "It's not about me anymore," and when they think less about "me" and more about "we."

Looking back, taking the promotion into leadership was actually a fortuitous coincidence when writing this book. Even though I knew what I was getting myself into, being a new leader was invaluable in writing this book for new leaders. Let the science, practice, and art I describe and present in this book give you a solid foundation to understand why, what, and how to be the boss everyone wants to work for.

It's time for you to flip your script. If you truly believe that you can, are 100 percent committed to flipping your script, and want to be the boss everyone wants to work for, this book is for you. Read on, and get ready to flip your script.

## chapter 2

# Flip Your Mindset

*I'm driving home Friday. I'm pumped about my raise. All these thoughts start going through my head, like, "How am I going to celebrate? What will I do with that extra money each paycheck? What new things will I buy? Maybe those golf clubs I've wanted." Then it hits me—I've got to lead people now. I've been an individual contributor all my working life. How do I suddenly start on Monday being a boss?*

I felt awesome driving home. It really was an honor that my organization wanted to promote me into a leadership role. And that the executive team and others in my organization thought that highly of me? Wicked awesome.

Being a boss was a new challenge for me. Yeah, I was hesitant. But I really was up for it. I've always been up for a challenge.

But I definitely had that "Oh *bleep*" feeling too. I knew that when I sat down at my desk on Monday, that comfortable feeling of being in control, responsible for me and my actions alone, and the confidence that I was pretty darn good at what

I did, would vanish. I knew that on Monday, something would be different. I had to be different.

So what did I do? I did what any highly motivated go-getter would do who wants to prove that he deserved the promotion into leadership.

I crammed.

I'll rephrase that. I seriously thought about cramming. I thought about pulling a couple all-nighters perusing all the blogs and reading all the pertinent journal articles possible, and ordering all the leadership books I could, with overnight delivery. I was going to cram like it was an exam I hadn't studied for. But preparing to be a boss by cramming and pulling all-nighters won't work for a new leader. Doing nothing with a "business as usual" outlook won't work either.

What will? Take a deep breath, and accept that as soon as you get promoted into your first leadership role, you aren't an individual contributor anymore. And flip your script. If you don't, your career is likely on a track to derailment.

## Derailment: Are You a Train or a Trainwreck?

We all know them—we've seen them walking in our organizations. We may even be one. Rock star. Golden child. High potential. Da bomb. We're kind of a big deal, as Ron Burgundy from the movie *Anchorman* puts it. People in our organizations with huge upside. Several of them make it as leaders and have successful careers.

But sometimes, for various reasons, some don't. They stopped progressing. They were demoted or fired. That's what derailment is, and I've been studying it at CCL since 2005. Morgan McCall and Michael Lombardo, well-known researchers at CCL, were among the first to uncover reasons why people derailed decades ago, and those reasons are still relevant today.[1] Be aware of these because they can get in the way of flipping your script and ruin your chances of being a boss everyone wants to work for.

### Reason 1: "$@#! Happens"

Some reasons leaders derail are beyond our control. For instance, "$@#! happens" with a downsizing, merger, reorganization, or bad luck. Things that have nothing to do with who we are, things that happened in our organization that we had no control over, derail our chances at being an effective leader.

But even when "$@#! happens" and you survived that downsizing or reorg, you may still derail because you failed to do something that you actually had control over. Many rock-star individual contributors derailed as leaders because they were set in their ways, unable to change and adapt to new surroundings, environments, and organizational or management culture. They didn't flip their script. As a new leader, adapt to changes that come your way, to avoid derailing.

### Reason 2: Success Goes to Our Heads

Because rock-star individual contributors lived the script that helped them become successful, they've hardly ever received negative feedback. They start believing in their own press clippings. They get big egos. They feel invincible. So, they become overly ambitious and unaware of the follow-through needed to move work toward completion or meet the obligations of the business. When some transition to leadership, where they can't rely on their successes, talent, skills, and technical savvy anymore, it all falls apart. They didn't flip their script. They derailed.

## Reason 3: Weaknesses Were Ignored and Never Addressed

Our own weaknesses play a huge role in derailment. Granted, these weaknesses may have been overlooked in the beginning. They may have even "worked" in the beginning. But over time, these weaknesses persisted, were ignored, never addressed, and eventually led to derailment.

Think about the person in your organization who is rather cold, arrogant, or insensitive. This individual doesn't handle conflicts well and can't build teams effectively. He or she is self-centered and gets things done by being insensitive, pushing others as hard as humanly possible, up to and beyond the tipping point. This person yells, screams, belittles, berates, and leaves a trail of bruised people behind. In the script of some individual contributors, bullying helped them become successful; it's how they made (and exceeded) the numbers and got ahead. And research sort of supports it. Gerald Ferris and his colleagues[2] believe bullying can be effective *at certain times* and *in certain situations* if used *infrequently, strategically,* and for *short-term improvements.* Bullying "immature" workers may force them to either "shape up" or, better yet, compel them to "ship out" so that the position can be filled with someone more appropriate, mature, or just plain easier to work with.

So does this mean the boss everyone wants to work for should bully others? No. Ferris and his colleagues also say emphatically that bullying is not effective in the long term and can cause a dysfunctional work environment. People who are bullied at work tend to feel less satisfied in their jobs; their health worsens; absenteeism rates rise; and they'll want to leave your organization for good. Further, the long-term effects of constant bullying lead to decreased motivation, morale, and satisfaction in jobs. All that bullying, pushing, and insensitivity is really part of a weakness some leaders may have. And bullying definitely won't work as leaders move up the organization, where artful influence, perspective taking, and political savvy are undeniably needed.

These leaders who bully clearly have problems with interpersonal relationships and are unable to build and lead teams. If these or other ignored weaknesses have been part of your script as an individual contributor, flip your script now.

## Reason 4: Strengths Became Weaknesses

Lastly, strengths people had as individual contributors may become weaknesses as they become leaders later. No doubt, we all must rely on our strengths, the things we are good at, the things that make us stand out from other people. Strengths are part of our script. They make us subject matter experts and specialists in our trade, and help us get promoted into leadership. For example, being independent is a strength many individual contributors have, and oftentimes part of our script.

But strengths like independence, which served us well as individual contributors, can become weaknesses later as leaders. For instance, new leaders must rely on others, work with others, and manage teams. Although you were being lauded for the independence that's part of your script as an individual contributor, as a new leader you will be criticized and vilified for your independence because it is nowhere in the script of a boss.

Derailment definitely went through my own head, as a new leader, before my "official" first day as a boss.

> *It's sort of ironic; I study derailment, and now that I'm a boss, I'm nervous it will happen to me. One of my strengths is my ability to do things on my own. I get things done by myself all the time. But as a new leader, if I really and truly intend to succeed at being a boss, I should let that go. I must work with others to accomplish some major things that I would never be able to do alone. If I try to do it by myself, I may start behaving like those derailed leaders I study.*

Maybe knowing all of these reasons could have helped Kurt avoid derailment.

## A Case Study in Derailment: Kurt the Expert

> *Kurt excelled in high school. He was in all sorts of extracurricular activities, got into a great college, graduated with honors, and got into his first choice for a graduate program. During an internship, he landed in a dream organization, and excelled at doing all the work he was assigned, and more. He continually went above and beyond what was asked and became known for things he'd always been given praise for his entire life: his confidence, discipline, drive, determination, rigor, attention to detail, strong work ethic, ambition, take-charge attitude, and technical ability. He was groomed to be a supervisor as soon as he finished his degree.*

*"It's a lock," Kurt thought. "They'd be stupid if they
didn't hire me. I'm productive. I get work done. All I have
to do is pass this simple little supervisor selection test. I just
have to say all the right things, answer all the questions
correctly. No problem."*

*Though he thought he knew all the answers, he failed
the test. He was shocked and dumbfounded. He asked his
boss and superiors what went wrong. "Kurt, you clearly
conveyed that you have the knowledge and skills to be a
great worker. But you fell short in telling us how you can
work well with others. You don't have the experience
beyond your job to understand how things work around
here and how relationships are so important. You didn't
convey how you can lead teams effectively and explain
how you can encourage, manage, and motivate others. You
just don't have enough experience being a supervisor, and
in all the things supervisors must do, in order to be a
supervisor."*

*Kurt's dream job was gone. There was no place else to go
in the organization. Eventually he had no choice but to
leave the organization.*

You can probably see how the behaviors and reasons people
derail all played out in Kurt's derailment. Kurt's ego got the
better of him. He clearly had knowledge and technical savvy.
But he wasn't able to show that he could cultivate relationships inside and outside his department. He couldn't get out
of his role as a great individual contributor and show how he
could work well leading teams and working with others up
and down the organization. His strengths as an individual
contributor clearly were weaknesses as a supervisor. He never
flipped his script.

Let Kurt's story be a warning sign that it can happen to anyone.

Even me.

I'm Kurt. I had my "dream job" all lined up for me out of graduate school. Yet I failed the supervisory selection test for all the reasons listed. And here is the humbling, ironic part. I failed a supervisor selection test made by a bunch of industrial-organizational psychologists. My degree? Industrial-organizational psychology. My major field of study? Leadership. So, I failed a test that in many respects I had the degree and education to actually make. Epic fail.

Out of graduate school, I was known for being bright, highly skilled, and a hard worker. The script obviously worked for me as an individual contributor. But my career stalled out and derailed at that organization because I thought I could just rest on that reputation. I didn't realize I had to flip my script.

Granted, some of you may be saying, "This isn't me, and it will never be me." You may be right. It's like what I've said in my research: about half of managers are effective in the workplace[3] and are great at what they do. They will never venture too far into the possibility of derailment.

Of course, if my research says 50 percent of managers are effective, that means the other 50 percent aren't. So some may be living in denial, on their way to derailment, and just don't know it yet. In my research, blind spots are relevant predictors of derailment potential, and it can happen to anybody. Let this be a public service announcement for you to flip your script to get off the track to derailment.

Others, however, may see it unfolding in front of them. You may feel helpless and demoralized because you do see the derailment signs. Is there hope? Emphatically, yes! With work, time, and support, you and anyone else who truly want to get off the track to derailment can. That's what the science, practice, and art behind this book are all about.

## Your Mindset Is a Terrible Thing to Waste

For all new leaders, let this be your wake-up call. If you truly want to be the boss everyone wants to work for, the first thing you need to do is flip your mindset.

### Why You Should Flip Your Mindset

In my latest research on nearly 300 new leaders, the most effective ones flipped their mindset.

First, I gathered performance ratings of each of the new leaders. Through CCL assessments, I asked the bosses of these new leaders how well they were doing on the job as new leaders, to understand who excelled and who struggled.

I also asked these new leaders a series of questions about their own motivation behind learning and development.[4] Now, we all have motivations, reasons why we want to learn something new. One of these is Charlie's main motivation:

*I want to learn because it will make me look good in front of others, especially my coworkers. It will really set me apart from everyone. I'll impress others with what I'm learning, and I'll get some great recognition too, which is pretty motivating.*

Now, there's nothing inherently wrong with this. We are all ambitious and seek personal excellence. For some of us, that's our major motivational factor for learning. For others, it's sort of in the background. But all of us have this motivation for learning to some degree or another.

There's a second motivation we all have, like the one Judy primarily feels:

*I want to learn because I find learning inherently satisfying. I really love to learn; it's so engaging to learn something new. It's fun. It's not really about me, my skills, my abilities, and wanting to impress others. No, I'm motivated to learn because of the joy that comes from it.*

Again, some of us feel this way a lot, some a little. But all of us have this motivation for learning to some degree or another.

So how do those two motivations play out for new leaders?

Let's first look at new leaders who were struggling and were ineffective in their jobs, according to their bosses. Their motivation to learn because it brought them recognition, made people aware of how good they were, and impressed others (like Charlie's major motivation) was more prevalent than the motivation to learn because it was fun, exciting, and engaging. It's like that old breakup line: "It's not you; it's me." And we know that's the script of individual contributors who want people to know how talented they are, drawing attention to their own abilities, achievements, and personal desire to get ahead. Their script stayed the same and never flipped when they transitioned into leadership. And the results suggest they weren't very successful.

And the new leaders who excelled? The ones with high performance ratings from their own boss? The opposite was true.

Their motivation to learn because it was fun, exciting, and engaging (like Judy's major motivation) far outweighed their motivation to learn because it would bring them rewards, recognition, and would impress others. They flipped their script by flipping their mindset.

Want to be effective as a new leader and be the boss everyone wants to work for? *My research on new leaders suggests that you flip your script by flipping your mindset. Be motivated to learn because it's fun, engaging, exciting, and you enjoy it.*

Some have found the importance of flipping your mindset. Carol Dweck is arguably best known for her book *Mindset*.[5] According to Dweck, there are two predominant mindsets. Some people have a fixed mindset (what some academics call entity theorists). They think what gets them ahead in life are their innate abilities, intelligence, talents, and hard work. They must constantly prove themselves to others. They want to look smart. They are motivated by extrinsic motives (external rewards, approval from others, wanting to look good in front of others, or wanting to prove they are better than others). They also have a fear of failure because failure says something negative about their abilities.

Others have a growth mindset (what some academics call incremental theorists). They think their abilities can be developed through learning, training, and persistence. They believe they can improve from their own failures. They want to learn because it's fun, engaging, intrinsically pleasing, and challenging. This attitude resembles a flipped script.

The research of Dweck and others clearly demonstrates the positive effects of a growth mindset in parenting, school, and relationships. And regardless of leadership experience, their research provides evidence that leaders with a growth mindset, a flipped script, are much better off than leaders with a fixed mindset.

For some, that's great news. You're convinced and ready to flip. But for others, you know yourself really well. You may believe you have a fixed mindset. It's probably impractical and unattainable to even try to flip. Are you stuck? Can you really flip your mindset? Yes, you can.

In one study, Peter Heslin, Don Vandewalle, and Gary Latham focused only on managers with a fixed mindset.[6] They purposefully split fixed-mindset managers into two groups, each taking a 90-minute workshop. The formats of the workshops were nearly identical, with one critical difference:

- One group's 90-minute workshop emphasized the fact that people have multiple abilities, and in some areas they are strong, whereas in other areas, they are weak.
- The other group's 90-minute workshop focused specifically on adopting a growth mindset through "self-persuasion." In that workshop, managers tried to talk themselves into adopting a growth mindset—in other words, flipping their mindset.

So what happened?

The fixed-mindset managers who attended the "self-persuasion" training (described in the second bullet point) were *more willing to provide coaching* and had *higher quantity and quality of performance improvement suggestions*. These changes were not seen in the fixed-mindset managers who attended the other workshop (described in the first bullet point).

If you think you have a fixed mindset, the research offers you hope. If given the proper time, energy, and support, you can flip your mindset. These studies point to three great things for you to remember as a new leader in flipping your mindset.

First, mindsets can be valuable to you as a new leader. Undoubtedly, mindsets have deep and positive effects on us.

Second, you can flip your mindset. You are not stuck with one mindset your entire life. Your brain is highly malleable, always forming new connections. You can learn new things and flip your mindset at any age if you work hard enough, focus hard enough, and want it badly enough.

Third, you need support. With enough time and support from others, you can flip your mindset. Support from people at work, and away from work, is an important factor in your own personal development. Leaders who report high levels of social support are better able to cope with hardships, overcome challenges, and learn and develop in their jobs.[7] Having support around you is crucial for you to flip your mindset.

## What You Can Do to Flip Your Mindset

The one big thing you can do to flip your script by flipping your mindset? It's your "mindchatter": talk to yourself differently. A lot of what Dweck, Heslin and his colleagues, and others recommend in flipping your mindset revolves around the voices that come from us—self-talk, or what I call "mindchatter." It's that inner dialogue we have providing us opinions and evaluations on how well (or not so well) we are at doing things. It's the play-by-play commentary. It's the positive, optimistic, and validating chatter we hear when we do something right. It's also the critical, harsh, crippling, destructive chatter we hear when we aren't at our best and are struggling.

Organizational psychologist Steven Rogelberg and his research team literally read what leaders told themselves, the mindchatter of 189 top executives who went through a leadership development program at CCL.[8] All of these leaders wrote a letter addressed to themselves that would be mailed to them weeks later. In the letters, the executives talked about goals they wanted to achieve, what they had learned in the program, their work and personal life issues, and their hopes for the future. Rogelberg and his team deconstructed the mindchatter in these letters and found a key difference between the type of mindchatter effective and ineffective executives have.

They first examined effective executives who were rated by their own followers and bosses as "outstanding" and "exceptional" at demonstrating leadership to others in providing support, mentoring, helpfulness, and collaboration. The mindchatter of these executives was constructive, insightful, self-reflective, motivational, and practical in nature. Interestingly, they tended to view themselves as being in better health too. Plus, they usually ended their letters on a positive, reassuring note, confident of their success in the future.

What about ineffective executives? Their mindchatter was destructive, more negative in nature. They didn't want to face the challenges ahead. Some were even afraid of challenges and failure. They were also pessimistic. Further, they tended to feel that job stress was affecting their health. And they usually ended their letters on a more depressing note, believing they wouldn't reach their goals.

I know it's tough. We all face doubt and uncertainty. We all have times when the voices in our head say something like, "I've never been a boss before. Can I do it?" Or, "I've never failed at anything. What happens if I fail at this?" Or worse, "I'm not good at this. I'll never be able to flip my script."

When things start to go sideways, we all tend to start focusing more on ourselves, our own talents, and keeping our egos in check. When you hear these sorts of lines in your head, recognize it's not the mindset of the boss everyone wants to work for. Shut it up. And flip it.

Mindchatter matters. As a new leader, make sure your mindchatter is constructive. Be perceptive, motivational, realistic, and positive. Listen to the right mindchatter. Use your mindchatter to tell yourself, "You can do it in time" or "You do have the power to learn about leading others" and "You can be the boss everyone wants to work for."

And it's really important to use "you," not "me."

## Even the Pronouns Matter

The nearly 300 new leaders in my study all took part in CCL's "Maximizing your Leadership Potential" program, a three-day leadership development course. Before they came to the program, they wrote a letter to themselves sort of like the executives did in the Rogelberg study. The difference? Instead of writing a letter to themselves in the future, these new leaders all wrote letters to their past selves. The instructions were:

> *You have learned many lessons since making the transition from an individual contributor to a manager. What do you now know about leading people that would have been helpful to have known at the time of that transition? Write yourself a letter, telling your earlier self those helpful leadership lessons.*

Consider this new leader in the construction industry:

*Since I became a leader, I've overcome many obstacles and learned many lessons. Some the hard way. I know that there are so many different personalities, and all have to be dealt with in a different way. My biggest lessons have come with the more sensitive people. But I realize I am so much better at dealing with them.*

*I have learned to listen to their needs even though I know what they are. I also need to give them the praise that they figured things out, even when I already knew. I have a long ways to go to be the great leader that I want to be, but I know I am on the right path.*

Now, look at this letter written by a new leader from the aerospace and defense industry:

*You've grown a lot over the past three years. As you've come to really know your position, you've adapted it to suit your strengths. You worked hard to make it your own. You've challenged yourself to be a team player and also a team leader. Though you've done so much to come into your own as a leader, it would have been easier if you had let your voice be heard earlier and louder. A weakness you've had, even since college, is to let others lead if you think they know more than you. However, to effectively lead others and shape situations, you must use your skills, be confident, and speak up!*

Undeniably, these leaders have great lessons for any new leader. But from a mindchatter perspective, did you notice the striking difference in pronoun usage? The focus of the mindchatter around the pronouns used, specifically, the first-person use of "I" and "me" pronouns versus the second-person "you" pronouns were quite different. And when I linked the amount of times those pronouns were used to performance ratings made by their coworkers, something very telling appeared.

New leaders who used the pronouns "me" and "I" more and more, like the person in the first example, were perceived by their peers as *more likely to derail* and their boss tended to rate them as *low performers.*

New leaders who used "you" more in their letters (like the second) were perceived by their peers as *less likely to derail.*

In her book, Carol Dweck discussed the "I" versus "you" pronoun among chief executive officers (CEOs), the people at the very top of organizations. CEOs who wanted validation—superstar or hero status, or wanted others to believe they were the smartest, most talented person in the room—tended to have a fixed mindset. They used the pronoun "I" more. Others mentioned in her book, like Jack Welch of GE, Anne Mulcahy of Xerox, or Lou Gerstner of IBM, had a growth mindset. They hated using the word "I" and preferred to use "you" or "we" or "us" in their writings and speeches. They also emphasized the importance of learning and growing as a leader, not being the smartest and best and brightest in the room. "It's not about me anymore," right? They got it. They flipped their script by flipping their mindset.

The research of Dweck and Rogelberg, as well as my own on new leaders, undeniably says our mindsets are powerful. Our mindchatter is powerful. What we think, the way we talk to ourselves, even drilled down to the smallest of pronouns we use in our own mindchatter, can predict our effectiveness as new leaders. Flip your script by flipping your mindset.

## Back to Kurt

This chapter provided examples, cautionary tales, and true-life stories of leaders who couldn't make it, those who did, and the scripts and mindsets they had. In closing, let's return to Kurt . . . I mean me.

First, know that just because you derail or feel you may be on a track toward derailment, your career and life aren't necessarily over. After coming to CCL, my career really flourished, and I became a director. Maybe you have suffered a demotion; maybe you had to leave your dream job. But, like me, you can make it someplace else.

But hear this too. When you get that second chance, flip your script, or a similar outcome will likely occur. Look at my own mindchatter:

> *I've had to flip my mindset, and it's been extremely difficult. My first gut instinct? Think of myself and what should be done for my own benefit. As a leader, though, you've had to purposefully flip your mindset and think less of "me" and more of others so the ending won't be the same. And when times get tough, or you don't quite know what to do, stay positive and use "you" to stay motivated.*

The takeaway from all of this?

The script you had as an individual contributor clearly worked for you because it got you your first leadership position. If you keep living that script over and over again as a new leader and still expect success, you are likely on the track to derailment.

Flip your mindset and you'll be off to a great start as you flip your script. Next on your agenda? Flip your skill set.

As a leader, it's not your technical skills that make you a success, but your personal skills. And they'll need developing. Concentrate, build, and develop skills that might not have been relevant to you as an individual contributor and technical expert, but that are now definitely needed as a new leader going forward.

**THE COACH'S CORNER—YOU CAN FLIP YOUR MINDSET**

Not all of us can have our own personal coach to help us flip our scripts. Well, this is the next best thing. Go to the companion website to further your learning and get more tips. For instance, in the resources page for this particular chapter, you'll read more about how to avoid derailment, and find more ways to help you flip your mindset.

And at the end of each chapter, I'll pose two questions for you to think about and two ways to put the work into action. These are meant to keep you engaged in the learning and give you support as you flip your script. Reading this book with a group of peers? Use this to start a dialogue to coach, mentor, develop, and support each other. What you can learn from your own personal reflections and your peers can be just as valuable as what you read.

Some of the following are based on "self-persuasion" and similar work that both Dweck and Heslin and his colleagues have conducted.[9] I hope it helps you flip your script by flipping your mindset.

**Question 1: What is your own experience?** Reflecting on your life experience can be a powerful way for you to flip your script. So, reflect on this: What are the reasons why it's important for you as a new leader to develop your abilities?

**Question 2: How did others flip their scripts?** Reflect on a time when you thought somebody couldn't do something, but the person persevered. Now that person is exceeding expectations. Maybe it's someone who was in a similar "new leader" situation, who eventually became a boss everyone wanted to work for. What did the person do to flip his or her script? What does it tell you about your ability to flip your script?

**Application 1: Role-play a conversation.** Have one of your friends, peers, mentors, or trusted colleagues play the role of a struggling direct report you manage. Listen to what this person is struggling with, and provide examples of how his or her abilities can be developed and improved. Sympathize, empathize, and bring up a time when you lacked ability at something before, but now you are excelling.

**Application 2: Write a letter to your past self.** Handwrite a letter to your past self, detailing what you know now about leading others that you wished you would have known then. What is it about leading people that would have been helpful to have known back then? Put what you learned about mindchatter to good use. Be constructive, insightful, self-reflective, motivational, confident, and practical. End on a positive, reassuring note. And don't use those "I" and "me" and "my" pronouns; use "you" and "your" in your letter and in your mindchatter going forward. Remember from the research, all of that matters and is linked to effective leaders.

## chapter 3

# Flip Your Skill Set

*So it's Monday. Same desk. Same computer. Same messy office I've been meaning to clean forever. But I'm different now—I'm a boss. I've got the mindset needed: "It's not about me anymore." I'm ready to learn what to do, not because it's going to make me look good, but because it will be fun and engaging. But what skills do I need to learn and develop to best lead, skills that will help me with my direct reports and serve my coworkers? I know all about downloading data, writing academic articles, and making data come alive in reports, but that has nothing to do with leading others. There are tons of skills new leaders need in order to be effective. Which ones should I focus on the most?*

That was my mindchatter on Monday at 7:45 A.M. Overwhelmed and lost. Again. But after I got my morning caffeine in my system, I told myself:

*Technical skills, knowing how to run statistical programs, crunching numbers, and writing reports won't help you as a*

51

*new leader. You need to trust the research you've done on new leaders. Trust what you learned from training other new leaders. You know what to do. Flip your skill set.*

## The Four Skills to Flip

As a new leader, when you get promoted to be a boss, it's not about having the skills of an individual contributor anymore. It's not about technical smarts and savvy, knowing the lingo, mastering the program, operating the machine, closing the sale, or having the work-arounds at your fingertips. Now, flip your skill set.

Books, webinars, blogs, news articles, experts, and talking heads in the media—so much is being said about the dozens of leadership skills all managers must have. All this information can be brain overload, and it's no wonder many new leaders are lost before they even get started. But why listen to talking heads and their inflated egos about what they think, when you can see what *actual new leaders* say? That's where the science really comes in handy.

Each of the new leaders I studied took a 360-degree assessment. It's a way to assess themselves and be assessed by their own bosses, peers, direct reports, or relevant others inside and outside the organization on how well or poorly they are performing in certain areas. That way, a leader gets to see a "360-degree view" of themselves from many different perspectives. It's pretty daunting and even scary, but a lot of great information comes from these assessments.

In my research, I explored their data in two key areas:

- *Importance:* What skills did new leaders and their coworkers think were most important for success as a leader in their organization?
- *Skill level:* How effective (or ineffective) were these new leaders at performing these skills?

First I looked at the importance data. If new leaders themselves and their own bosses, peers, and direct reports think some skills are more important than others, that's great information to know. When it comes down to it, it's probably a waste of time to focus on building skills that are not that relevant to success. So, narrowing down the focus to the skills everyone says are important for success—that's a good place to start.

Second, I looked at skill level, especially how effective—or in this case ineffective—new leaders are at those same important skills. If, across the board, new leaders are relatively strong at something, should we throw more time, money, and effort in building that up? Probably not. Remember the research; strengths overplayed and overused can eventually derail your career. So then I started looking at the weaknesses, because unaddressed weaknesses can derail your career.

Over and over again, four skills kept coming to the surface. The following four skills were consistently picked as being more important for success than others as well as being skills new leaders often struggled with more than others:

- Communication
- Influence

- Leading team achievement
- Developing others

If it's highly important for success, and not many new leaders are good at it, that's a skill gap worth closing.

When I ran the numbers, I vowed from that moment on I would tell the new leaders I trained to flip their skill set with those four skills to be the boss everyone wants to work for. And at 7:46 A.M. that Monday morning, sitting at my desk, I also made a commitment to better myself in these four key areas.

In this chapter, I'll cover communication and influence specifically and leave the other two skills for later chapters.

## Communication—It's More Than Words

I remember sitting in my house around the end of 2008, flipping through the channels. One of the business channels had Warren Buffett on it. I tuned in because I wanted to learn how to make billions of dollars like he did. But the show was all about MBA students asking Buffett questions. One student asked, "What courses are MBA schools currently lacking in teaching their students?" Without hesitation, Buffett said, "Communication." He said the same thing in a town-hall meeting a year later.[1]

The importance of communication was not lost on one of the richest people in the world. It shouldn't be lost on you either.

But what is it about communication for new leaders? It's not what you say, it's how you say it.

## Why You Should Flip Your Communication Skill Set

Think about it. As an individual contributor, people look at your work. As a new leader, people look at you—your face, body language, behaviors, and actions. Your ability to communicate with others is valued and relevant in accomplishing your work and connecting with your direct reports and other coworkers. Communication is a big portion of your job.

The data give more evidence. Each of the new leaders I studied provided answers to this question: "What are the three most critical leadership challenges you are currently facing?" When we examined these challenges, 17.6 percent of new leaders said communication in some form or another was one of their top challenges.[2] For instance, one woman in the government sector said one of her biggest challenges was "getting my point across in an effective manner." Or take this man in the construction industry who said it pretty plain and simple:

*Effective communication! How to effectively tell them what to do without saying, "Because that's what I said."*

Communication is such a broad topic. But the one area I consistently tell new leaders to understand, enhance, and improve when it comes to communication is nonverbal communication—whether it's getting your point across, tailoring your communication to your audience, or saying something other than "Because that's what I said." Ironically, the type of communication that has nothing to do with words—that is, "nonverbals"—makes all the difference.

When you are talking with others in the hallway, during one-to-one meetings or presentations, or anywhere else at work,

### IT'S NOT WHAT YOU SAID—IT'S HOW YOU SAID IT

Imagine two different bosses. Each is getting some coffee at the machine in the break area. Both see a direct report who has a major problem with a project at work coming straight to them. The direct report briefly explains the problem and wants a little bit of the boss's time to talk about what to do next and how to solve it.

Both bosses then say the exact same words after the problem is explained: "You know I always have an open-door policy. Come to my office when you are free, and we can discuss your concerns."

One boss puts cream in the coffee and says these words very quickly, not really looking at the direct report, expressionless, and then starts to walk away while saying those words.

The other puts the cup down and says the words in a gentle manner, looking concerned and squaring up to talk, looking the direct report in the eye.

Which direct report do you think will actually feel welcomed enough to go see the boss?

The words, what many people think communication really is all about, were exactly the same. But the actions, and meaning behind them, were so different. This example may be extreme, but not out of the ordinary, particularly for new leaders.

are you really "saying" what you think you are saying? The actual "words" said really make up a small portion of what's actually being said. Science agrees. Researchers Ray Bird-whistell[3] and Albert Mehrabian[4] believed that nonverbal communication makes up anywhere between 65 and 93 percent of the total emotional interaction between two people. We tend to pay attention more to the nonverbals—that is, the behaviors—than to the verbals, the words. And when the words don't match the behaviors? We believe what's not being said, the nonverbals, rather than the words. Even the smallest, faintest nonverbal signal or behavior that is not aligned with the conversation, situation, or words can confuse your audience and lessen your credibility and your coworkers' confidence, faith, and trust in you as a leader.

Leaders who haven't flipped their script don't understand that. Their main priority is usually just getting their message—the words—across. They probably aren't as concerned with how it's being heard, or as receptive to what people think.

Be the boss everyone wants to work for, and flip your script by flipping your communication. Your nonverbals and how you say your words add credibility to what you say. And by reading the nonverbals of others, you will get your point across better. In fact, the science and research shows the connection between poor nonverbal communication and ineffective leadership. Consider these examples:

- Leaders who display improper eye contact are seen as ineffective.[5]
- Leaders who are not clear, fluent, and articulate with their words are judged as ineffective and less credible.[6]
- Individuals with unsteady eye contact, unvaried voice modulation, inappropriate affect, and low energy level in hand gestures, smiles, and body movement were judged as possessing low leadership potential.[7]
- Touching your hands, touching your face, crossing your arms, and leaning back are all tied to perceptions of

untrustworthiness. We all know how important trust is in leadership. And here's the kicker—when a robot made those gestures and postures, that robot was seen as untrustworthy, according to research led by David DeSteno.[8] Think about that. If we are labeling a robot—something nonhuman, with no feelings or emotions—as untrustworthy based on nonverbals, think of how powerful those nonverbals can be to describe you, a human being who actually leads others.

## What You Can Do to Flip Your Communication Skill Set

It's what I tell new leaders all the time when I talk about the importance of communication: *As a leader, you are never not communicating.* Even when you are not saying a word, you are saying something with your actions and behaviors, whether you know it or not. Your nonverbals affect how you are seen as a leader. So to flip your communication skill set, be aware of every type of way you communicate nonverbally. These ways are what psychologists Steve Nowicki and Marshall Duke,[9] among others, term different "channels" of nonverbal communication. Marshall and I believe it is especially significant for leaders to understand these six channels.[10] To flip your communication skill set, here are the six.

**1. Rhythm and use of time: not just for music.** Rhythm plays a role in the way you communicate with others. Being "out of sync" with others may cause confusion, anxiety, or discomfort for both you and the other person or people you are with. Your use of time is closely related to rhythm. How you organize time and commitments says a lot about you. No words said, but you are communicating something about yourself and others just based on how you treat the aspect of time. Consider coming into a meeting five minutes late. You may be telling people your time is more valuable than theirs without saying one word.

**2. Interpersonal distance (space) and touch: not about being touchy-feely.** This channel deals with boundaries or territories around us. According to anthropologist Edward Hall,[11] our "personal space" is sort of an imaginary, flexible bubble around us, bigger in the back than the front, which grows or shrinks depending on the situation we are in, whom we are talking to, and the culture we are living in. There are several "zones" we use for communication, and if someone invades a zone and the rules that are part of them, that causes problems. So, standing too close to someone you don't know well (like the "close talker" from the TV show *Seinfeld*) may be irritating or somewhat intimidating.

Touch is on the extreme end of the "intimate zone" of interpersonal space. For friends and family, touch is usually meant to convey liking or love. In the workplace, touch carries extreme meanings and should definitely be used with caution. You don't want a lawsuit on your hands, or a negative reputation (i.e., being that person who gives people the creeps).

**3. Objectics: more than "dress for success."** A nonverbal channel that you may overlook at times, yet equally effective at telling people things about you without saying a word, is objectics. Think about your clothes, hair, tattoos, jewelry, cosmetics, and fragrance. Many times, it's the first thing people notice about you, and these objectics may tell people a lot about you in that split second: who you are, what you do, what you believe in, what you support, and your own personal values. And you didn't even say one word.

The dress code at work tells us what to wear. And though the style of dress may communicate to others your fashion sense, it may not be acceptable at work. But even if you follow the dress code, the way you wear your clothes tells people something about you. An unwrinkled shirt, pressed pants, clean lines, fitted clothes, color coordination, polished shoes, and styled hair sends the message that you are organized, neat, efficient, and confident. Messed-up hair and wrinkled clothes that are untucked, stained, mismatched, or inappropriate may tell others you don't take the time to take care of yourself. Think about what fragrances or colognes you use (and how much), how much makeup you may use, the height of your heels, or how you keep your moustache, beard, van dyke, goatee, or soul patch groomed. When it comes to communication, you definitely are what you wear and how you look.

**4. Gestures and postures: you reveal a lot with your hands and stance.** A fourth channel of nonverbal communication is gestures and postures. You can say a lot with your hands and body without uttering a single word: a wave hi, for example, or raising your hand to stop something. You can tell people what you think by shaking your head in a certain direction, or that you have no clue by shrugging your shoulders. These and other gestures can say a lot without speaking one word.

Your posture can say things as well. If you have a slouched posture, people may think you are tired or disinterested. Hands in pockets may convey boredom. But standing straight may tell others you are attentive, excited, enthused, or confident. Leaning in may tell someone you are interested in what is being said.

Have you seen the popular TED Talk by social psychologist Amy Cuddy?[12] If not, watch it. In both her talk and her book *Presence*,[13] Dr. Cuddy exposes how posture and "power posing" can greatly affect how we feel and act as leaders. The way you stand, like making yourself "big" or standing like Wonder Woman—all of that can communicate so much about you and can even make you feel powerful and enthusiastic as a leader.

**5. Facial expressions: you can read it all over my face.** In face-to-face interactions, a smile, frown, grimace, raising your eyebrows, eye contact—all of that can tell people something that words may not. It is true that the eyes are the windows to the soul. Like when you smile. Yes, of course, the corners of the mouth turn up. But many times, you fake a smile, and people know you are not sincerely happy. Why? When you genuinely smile, what is called a "Duchenne smile" (after its discoverer, Guillaume Duchenne) the "crow's-feet" (the "crinkles") around the eyes appear, and the pupils of the eyes may be dilated. When you fake a smile, none of that shows up.

**6. Paralanguage: say what?** The sixth nonverbal communication channel is paralanguage, or all the things that make up the sound that accompanies the words. Think about your tone of voice. The loudness, speed, and intensity of your speech. Silence (or absence of it) too. And don't forget those "credibility killers" that ruin your credibility, authority, and reputation, like, well, "like" and "you know" and "uh" and "um." All of these examples are part of paralanguage.

Think about the sentence "I need the report today." Emphasizing or stressing one word in that sentence may totally change the meaning. If you emphasize "I," you are clearly telling someone whom the report is for. If you stress "today," you are clearly telling someone the time urgency of the matter. If you say "Um, like, I need the report, by, like, today," well, how

**NONVERBAL COMMUNICATION IS BOTH GLOBAL AND LOCAL**

Nonverbal communication is hard enough when you are thinking about how to say the right thing. Now add on the cultural contingencies behind nonverbal communication, and it becomes even harder. Some nonverbals span the globe, but others are culturally distinct. Knowing these nuances can help you be a better boss with your global colleagues. Not knowing them can make you look like a naïve and uncultured wannabe or, worse, negatively affect your authority and ability to lead others.

When it comes to nonverbal communication and culture, the saying really is true: "When in Rome, do as the Romans do." If you are going somewhere new or meeting people from another part of the world, look up customs, what to do, not to do, and nonverbals that are offensive or off-limits in books that specialize in that country, area, or region. Or ask people who have recently been there or are natives to get insight. For more information, read books by authors Roger Axtell, Terri Morrison and Wayne Conaway, Stella Ting-Toomey, or the work of Don Prince and Michael Hoppe of CCL.[14]

credible do you sound? The entirety of the emotional meaning, interpretation, and credibility of what was said can change just based on paralanguage.

So now you know the six nonverbal channels and how they can communicate to people so much more than the words that you say. But to truly flip your script when it comes to your communication skill set, you realize "It's not about me anymore." So how do you put it into practice? Follow the platinum rule.

## The Platinum Rule of Communication

Even though flipping your communication sounds easy, we know it's difficult. The reason why it's so difficult may go back to what we've been told our entire lives. My mom (maybe yours too) told me to live by the golden rule—you know, "Treat others the way you want to be treated."

The golden rule can be applied to communication. Maybe your style of communication is to keep things at a bare minimum. All you want are the facts and nothing else. As humans, we tend to do what's natural and comfortable for us. So, as a new leader, you will tend to have those same, straight, to-the-point conversations when you're the boss. Why? Because it's the natural and preferred way you like to be communicated with. It's the golden rule: communicate with others the way you want to be communicated with.

In my time reading, writing, and researching new leaders, training them, and being one, I've realized the golden rule doesn't work when it comes to all things leadership. Flip it to the platinum rule:

Treat others the way *they* want to be treated.

It's a subtle difference, but so important. And it can greatly help new leaders flip their script, communicate better, and be the boss everyone wants to work for.

The platinum rule is a good tool to remember when you communicate with others. Say you only want to hear the bare minimum. You'll tend to converse with others in that manner too. But others (possibly the people who report to you) have a desire to hear more and be engaged in conversations and decisions. They want to be heard. So, flip your script by flipping your communication. Talk with others more, understand what others are feeling, and become more aware of the verbal and, in particular, nonverbal messages.

New leaders who have flipped their script by flipping their communication skill set get this point. With their flipped script, their mindchatter may be:

> *It's no longer about "me" and being the center of attention. It matters less the way "I" like to communicate and the words said. So shine the spotlight on the people you are communicating with. Pay attention to how you are saying those words with your nonverbals and how the message is being received. It's the platinum rule: communicate with others the way they want to be communicated with.*

Maybe you've gotten feedback or simply know that communicating with others isn't your strong suit. It's hard enough saying what needs to be said. Now there's all this other nonverbal stuff. Maybe you still haven't gotten over that presentation or speech you bombed. It's okay—we've all been there. Regardless of your past, you now are a new leader who can and will flip your communication skill set. You have the power to do it. Here are several pieces of research-based advice to help.

**Communication is giving and receiving at the same time.**
You know the six channels. But it's more than just knowing them. You must display or send messages nonverbally, and do so correctly and genuinely. That's what communication experts call "expressive nonverbal communication"—it's the ability to express, produce, and send any or all nonverbal behaviors to others.[15]

But it's not that simple either. Those same experts agree that you must also attend to "receptive nonverbal communication"— that's the ability to recognize, understand, and interpret the nonverbal behaviors of others.

Leaders who have not flipped their script tend to just focus on the words they are saying, trying to get their message across. They are neither concerned about how their nonverbals reinforce or emphasize their words and their message, nor by how it's received by reading the nonverbals of others. But what if you did flip your script? Your mindchatter may be something like this:

> *Be aware of the messages you are sending nonverbally.*
> *Understand how your message is being heard by reading*
> *the nonverbals of others. Adjust your nonverbals if your*
> *message isn't connecting. Your nonverbals strengthen*
> *your message and add credibility to what you are sending.*

Flipping your script by flipping your communication is tough. But with the proper time, attention, energy, and support, it's possible.

**Your "resting" face and body.**  Leaders who have flipped their script also understand they send messages when they are not saying one word, when they are at "rest." Here's my story.

> *While I was an individual contributor, I received feedback on how "serious" and at times, "intimidating" I was when someone came to my desk. I always had a "furrowed brow" and "squinted eyes" and "crossed arms." I got feedback saying, "You look focused, really busy and unapproachable." I was also told, "Bill, you don't really smile much; it's not very inviting." I also heard, "Bill, you talk really loudly, and it's distracting." In fact, as a joke, one person made a sign that said "!WARNING! Loud Talking in Progress" and made it a point to walk to my cube and put it up every time I talked on the phone. The person was about 50 feet away from me. I was that loud.*
>
> *I actually got those same pieces of feedback about my nonverbals from three separate people on three separate occasions.*

Such feedback has been tremendously helpful for me personally to flip my script by flipping my communication. As I said before, "you are never not communicating," and it showed! But here's the ironic part. All those nonverbals about me being "serious" and "intimidating" and "unapproachable" and "not very inviting" are all parts of my normal "resting" nonverbals. Our faces, our bodies, our voices naturally have a way they look and sound when we are not paying attention to them. That was all mine. I own it. When I'm not thinking about it, I cross my arms (because it's comfortable for me), I squint my eyes and furrow my brow, and I'm naturally just a loud guy. It's just what I do when I'm not thinking. It's what is natural to me. But remember, when you flip your script, "It's not about me anymore," right?

So when I became a boss, I knew I had to flip. I now make a conscious effort to open my eyes wider whenever someone approaches me. I purposefully try to uncross my arms and be more open in my posture when talking to people. I try to speak a little more softly. And I try to smile more because recent research by Dana Joseph and colleagues found 25 studies that connected happiness with positive leadership outcomes.[16] I even smile a real, genuine smile, not a fake one, when I greet someone or even when I'm about to call someone on the phone. Why?

**Emotions are contagious.** How you feel can impact those you lead. Some of this can be traced way back to Charles Darwin himself. This century, a 2011 review article led by Rashimah Rajah[17] listed more than 10 articles published in the first decade of the 2000s about emotions being contagious. Each of these studies connected a leader's positive affect with positive outcomes, including the mood and resilience of followers and a leader's own effectiveness. In 2013, Victoria Visser and her colleagues[18] found that when leaders displayed happiness, they were seen as more effective.

Though fewer in number, Rajah and colleagues also listed studies inspecting negative affect, with predictable results— leaders with negative emotions have followers who feel bad. And when you are stressed, the people around you will feel stressed as well.

The people you interact with, the people you lead and serve, all feed off of your emotions. So flip your script. Be

**YOUR EMOTIONS AND HOW YOU FEEL CAN AFFECT THE HEALTH OF OTHERS TOO**

These positive and negative interactions won't just affect you and how you are perceived as a leader. They can potentially affect the health and well-being of the people you interact with and lead. In a 2015 study, Jennifer Wong and Kevin Kelloway[19] hooked up blood pressure monitors to care workers in nursing homes. Every hour the monitor took a reading, and the workers answered items on a questionnaire, including whether or not they talked with their boss, and if so, how positive or negative that interaction was. Interestingly, when these workers had a negative interaction with their boss, their blood pressure went up, and it stayed elevated even when they got home. There's a real health cost when workers have negative interactions with their boss. The emotions you have as a leader and how you interact with your direct reports, staff, and team members truly have a lasting effect on them, even their health.

mindful of what you feel and how you are expressing those feelings at all times, because your emotions affect more than just you.

**Feel what others feel: build your empathy.** When you flip your script by flipping your communication skill set, pay attention to what's being said, and more importantly what's *not* being said, by the other person. You should be in tune with, understand, and relate to the thoughts, feelings, emotions, and experiences of your direct report, staff, team members, coworkers, and customers, and possibly even be moved to help them. That's what empathy is all about, and you should have it. And my own research illustrates that empathy is tied to a leader's success. Flipping your script by paying less attention to your own emotions and more to others' can help your career.

In a study of over 6,000 managers from 38 different countries, we found that managers displaying more empathy were rated by their own bosses as better performers. And while displaying empathy was positively related to performance around the world, in some countries like China, Egypt, Hong Kong, Malaysia, New Zealand, Poland, Singapore, and Taiwan, empathy had an even stronger positive relationship with performance.[20]

Further, in a 2015 study of managers in Australia,[21] we discovered a relationship between empathy and derailment potential—leaders who displayed less empathy tended to have a high potential to derail, according to their bosses and peers. And for leaders who displayed a lot of empathy, the opposite was true: they were perceived as having a low potential to derail. Interestingly, we also found that empathy was important for men and just as important, if not more so, for women. Man or woman, the ability to empathize with others matters to your present performance and future career as a leader.

Communication is one of the biggest skill gaps new leaders have. And for good reason—it's tough to flip your script when it comes to your communication. So, what if you don't? Well, think about the person who works for a leader who hasn't flipped his script. What would that person say about

**LISTEN UP!**

Can you understand another person's perspective? Do you pay attention to what your direct reports, boss, coworkers, or customers are saying to you? One great way to enhance your empathy skill is to listen better. Professors Kyle Brink and Robert Costigan[22] discovered listening as the most important oral communication skill in the workplace, more important than conversing or even presenting. Yet, only 11 percent of the business schools in their study listed listening as a learning goal, way fewer than those who listed presentation skills (76 percent). Listening in the workplace is a skill gap that all leaders should address, especially new leaders learning to develop others.

To enhance your empathy, listen better. Practice active listening. The Coach's Corner and the resources on the companion website give quick tips and advice to enhance your active listening.

the leader's communication? Probably things that closely resemble comments from coworkers of the new leaders I researched:

*He needs to be more engaged in conversation. If he's frustrated, it spills over into his attitude and optimism. . . . He needs to pay more attention to people when communicating. Stop being distracted. Be more empathetic. . . . Some of us feel intimidated by him because we don't understand him and because the way he communicates mistakes comes across as a bit abrasive in his tone and mannerisms. . . . He usually takes center stage when he talks. A better strategy to communicate is to listen more than speak.*

Is this the type of boss you want to be? Flip your script and be the boss everyone wants to work for by flipping your communication.

## Influence—"Do It Because I'm The Boss" Is Not Your Only Option

Influence is all about your power, authority, and ability to shape or change your audiences' actions, decisions, or opinions. Influence happens all the time at work. If you influence well, you'll be successful at work. But as you will read, influence is more than just "Do it because I'm the boss."

### Why You Should Flip Your Influence Skill Set

In 2003, Chad Higgins and his colleagues[23] looked at 31 studies about influence at work, and found certain influence tactics were consistently related with work outcomes. Specifically, ingratiation (getting people to like you or making people feel good about you by acting friendly and respectful or giving compliments) and rationality (using data, facts, figures, information, and logic to support your opinion) were both tied to how you are evaluated in your job. Specifically, those who tend to influence through ingratiation and rationality tactics are likely evaluated as better job performers.

Up to this point, you've probably used ingratiation and rationality pretty well. But as a new leader, that script must flip. Influence isn't about getting what you need for your own success. "It's not about me anymore." Flip your script.

As a new leader, your influence is essential in many different ways. You'll use it to carry out decisions. To obtain support for your ideas or vision. To acquire the necessary resources to get work done. You'll need to influence others to make their work easier and increase their dedication.

## What You Can Do to Flip Your Influence Skill Set

As the boss, you have one huge influence tactic in your possession. That "supervisor" or "manager" or "director" or similar title you possess gives you a natural power base to influence certain people, especially the ones who directly report to you. Using threats, rewards, and your own authority—the "Do it because I'm your boss and I said so" influence tactic—is appropriate and totally in line with getting work done. But there's a catch. Using that all the time will demotivate others. Plus, you really can't use that line with your peers, your own boss, upper management, and others across your organization because, well, you're not the boss of them. So what else is there?

Gary Yukl has studied influence for more than three decades. He has a taxonomy of 11 different influence tactics[24] that range from using flattery (part of ingratiation pointed out earlier) to using threats (i.e., pressure). If you want a deeper understanding of each of these 11 tactics, I highly recommend reading his work.

I will admit, 11 tactics may seem overwhelming as a new leader. So I'll try to make it a little more straightforward and simple. It's the "3 H's," and luckily they correspond to different body parts (figuratively speaking, of course), which makes them a bit easier to remember and apply.

*Head*—Influence people using rational approaches. Use your intellect, reason, logical arguments, and facts.

*Heart*—Influence people using emotional appeals. Let people know how a decision will affect their own lives, work, values, beliefs, or those of the people around them.

*Hands*—Influence people using a connection you have with them. Work together to accomplish a common goal.

So now you know three ways that you can influence others. The one big takeaway to flip your script by flipping your influence skill set? Follow the platinum rule—influence others the way they want to be influenced.

## The Platinum Rule of Influence

Suppose you are a new leader who likes to be influenced (or even energized) through facts, figures, and data (through the "head"). Your natural way to influence others is probably through the use of those same facts, figures, and data. The golden rule would say: Influence others the way you want to be influenced. But just as with communication, as a new leader, flip it. The platinum rule states: Influence others the way *they* want to be influenced.

Though you may love talking about data, others may be bored to tears when they hear it. Maybe that's the way you've done it before, and your influence attempts fell short. Now is your chance to flip your influence skill set by talking about values, beliefs, and feelings ("heart") or through reciprocity and collaboration ("hands").

"Do it because I said so" won't cut it anymore. But now you have several different ways to influence people. So just pick your favorite one and go, right? Leaders who didn't flip their script would do just that. And if you keep living that script, people will be disengaged and you won't have buy-in for your decisions.

But you know better! Remember: "It's not about me anymore."

The best way to flip your influence skill set is to understand your audience and influence them the way *they* want to be influenced. The next time you must influence someone or an audience, whether it is in a formal presentation to a group of people, a team meeting, or a one-on-one conversation, flip your script by flipping your influence skill set.

Need to influence through the head? Well, be specific and practical, and offer sensible goals. Are you providing step-by-step detail? Are you providing the numbers, the evidence?

Is your audience more likely to be influenced through the heart? Think about what you can do to build connections through harmony and teamwork. How can you passionately share your vision and link it with a person's own values and beliefs? How can you tell someone he or she is capable of what you are asking? What are ways to tap into a person's sense of service or desire to be attached to an outcome?

Is it going to be best to influence through the hands? Then ask, "What can we do so that both of us get something out of it?" How would you consult with others who have a lot of power, to get their buy-in or speak on your behalf? What sort of ideas can you bring to the table that you can offer a person in return for doing something for you?

I hope the takeaways with these two skills make it easier for you as a new leader. They are especially important in your relationships with others, discussed in the next chapter.

**THE COACH'S CORNER—YOU CAN FLIP YOUR SKILL SET**

Go to the companion website, and in the resources page for this chapter you'll find content including ways to improve your ability to express and receive the correct nonverbal behaviors, and information on how to build an "influence plan" to maximize your efforts to influence others.

Here are two questions and two applications for you to help you flip your skill set.

**Question 1: Do you *hear* or do you *listen*?** Think about the times you've gotten feedback about not listening. What were you doing (or not doing) when you got called out for not listening? What are the ways, through your nonverbals, that you can show others you are listening to them and paying attention?

**Question 2: Who is a master influencer?** Think about the leader in your organization who has the reputation of being able to influence others really well and get buy-in from everyone. What does that person do to build and maintain that reputation of being a great influencer?

**Application 1: Videochat and get feedback.** Many of us don't know how we come across in conversations and communication. So, Skype or FaceTime with a peer, a fellow new leader, or a trusted colleague, for ten minutes every week for the next ten weeks. Record the sessions, if you can. After each session, get this person's feedback on all six of your nonverbal channels. It will be uncomfortable, but worth it. You won't know what you are good at, bad at, or what you should change, until you hear it from someone (and if recorded, you can see it yourself).

And return the favor. Give these people insights on their nonverbals to help them flip their script by flipping their communication.

**Application 2: Write out and practice influence through a head, heart, and hands tactic.** Think about a current situation where you must influence someone. Write out a head, heart, and hands influence tactic. Then decide which tactic you think would be best for that person. Remember: influence others the way they want to be influenced. Once you decide, stand in front of a mirror, and practice influencing that person with that one particular tactic. The more you practice, the more comfortable you will be when it's go-time.

If you turn your attention to how someone else wants to be communicated with and wants to be influenced—instead of just relying on "my" way of doing things—you are on your way to flipping your script.

## chapter 4

# Flip Your Relationships

*It's still Monday, not even lunch yet. Geez, I'm hungry. And this meeting isn't helping my appetite either. I really wanted to use my communication and influence skills to help set a good impression as I was introduced as a new leader. I was excited to help set a new course and direction for our group's work. But then I heard, "You all don't understand. You all need to do things differently. You all are not providing the things we need." Wait, did I just hear, "You all?" I worked side by side with these people on Friday, and now I'm, "You all" less than 72 hours later? That was quick. They really see me differently. And, well, they are different too, now that I think about it. Today I'm the boss of people who were peers and friends Friday. What do I do about these relationships?*

Mid-morning on Monday, my first day as a boss, that's what I felt. I walked right into a buzz saw that I didn't expect. I've known these people, worked alongside them. They know me and know what I can do. Why didn't I get more credit? Why didn't they give me the benefit of the doubt that I have their best interest in mind?

It may not feel like a ton of bricks falling on your head, as it did for me. But clearly, even though the people have stayed the same, your relationship with all of them is different now that you are their boss. As I tell the new leaders I train:

> *When you officially become part of management, you start wearing the imaginary T-shirt that says, in big bold letters, "Leader" across your chest and the imaginary hat that has "Boss" stitched in, and everybody can spot your new wardrobe. Once that happens, people immediately see you differently. Adjust, get used to it, and flip your script.*

As an individual contributor, you get rewarded for focusing on yourself, like that old breakup line, "It's not you; it's me." That script worked. It's how you got this boss gig.

But as a new leader, you now get rewarded for shining the spotlight on others and making others your priority. When you flip your script by flipping your relationships, you now pay attention to others, their needs, and their well-being. Although that's never really a part of the individual contributor's script, relationships are a major part of your script as a new leader. There are two major relationships you have to flip: one with your peers (some, your friends) and one with your team.

## From BFF to Boss

I really had to start from zero. My work and reputation as an individual contributor did nothing for my former peers. I was "with them" before, and now I have to continually convince them they are my priority. I had to flip my script by flipping my "peer-to-boss" and in some cases, "BFF (best friend forever)-to-boss" relationship.

## Why You Should Flip Your BFF-to-Boss Relationship

Among the nearly 300 new leaders in my research study, the challenge most often mentioned was a relationship issue: "adjustment to people management and displaying authority." Almost 60 percent of new leaders mentioned it as one of their biggest challenges. Many new leaders have difficulties with moving from a coworker to a boss role. You were BFFs yesterday, and you are their boss today. How can you gain respect and still maintain the personal relationships you value? If that sounds familiar, you can feel the pain of this man who works at a nonprofit:

*I feel like I'm being taken advantage of because of my previous relationships with some members of my team. Sometimes I feel that people don't take tasks and projects as seriously as they should because they think they can use their friendly relationship with me to their advantage. It's difficult drawing that line because we were all at the same level. It's hard for me adjusting to managing people who were my coworkers, some my close friends.*

Many new leaders have difficulty displaying authority, particularly to those with whom they have a history and friendship. It's the biggest challenge new leaders have according to my research, and many just don't know how to go about flipping that relationship.

## What You Can Do to Flip Your Relationships with Your Former Peers (or BFFs)

We all need friends—even at work. We may call them BFFs (Taylor Swift has them) or "besties" (like Amy from the TV show *The Big Bang Theory*), or we may have our own Wolf Pack (who wouldn't want to hang out with Alan and others from the movie *The Hangover*?). Friends are significant. Even one of the biggest television shows in the history of mankind was about the topic, so it's hugely important, right?

Abraham Maslow famously said that a sense of belonging, the need for friendship, is a basic human need. Only food, water, and safety are more important. That sense of belonging, having friends at work in particular, carries great benefit. Studies show that people who have a best friend at work are more likely to report positive outcomes.[1] Karen Jehn and Priti Pradhan Shah imply that groups of friends tend to communicate more, provide more encouragement, and possess higher levels of commitment, and they are more cooperative than strangers or acquaintances.[2] Or, as Christine Riordan and Rodger Griffeth argue, when we believe we have the opportunity to make friends at work, we tend to identify with our work more, feel more involved and satisfied with our jobs, and become more committed to our organizations.[3]

Clearly, we need friends; they benefit us as well as our organizations. As an individual contributor, it's only natural you made friends at work.

But as a new leader, you may be managing those same friends. Awkward. So what do you do to flip these relationships in your new role as their boss? Flip your script. Here are four ways to get you started.

**Be clear.** Unless there is a clear written rule in your HR handbook against it, yes, you can still be friends. But both you and your friend-turned-subordinate must realize that your work relationship has changed. It's your job as the boss to talk about the new responsibilities you face in your new role and to set clear expectations and boundaries from the start. Explain that you are accountable for the development and performance of everyone who reports to you, not just your BFFs. The amount of time you spend with your friend-turned-subordinate and the nature of your interaction will probably change, so make that clear to your BFF.

Have this conversation as soon as possible. Get any issues you or your friend-turned-subordinate has out in the open. Talk about your expectations of him or her. And remember, communication is a two-way street. Listen to any expectations your friend has of you as the boss. Discuss where there is agreement or why there are discrepancies, if any.

**Be aware.** When you have that imaginary "Boss" hat and "Leader" T-shirt on that everyone can see, all eyes are on you. People will observe, notice, and go so far as to scrutinize every decision you make (or don't make), and whom you give your time and attention to (or whom you don't). Be aware of what you are doing and not doing.

The idea that you may give your friend-turned-subordinate more than you give others (or even that it's perceived that way) may come as a shock. But it's only natural to give more to those you know and trust. We're human; that's what humans do. However, success in your new leadership role is due in part to an understanding and awareness of the unique relationship you have with *each* of your direct reports, BFF or otherwise.

This is based on one of the major theories in leadership research: Leader–Member Exchange (LMX) theory. It's been around since the 1970s and proposes leadership as a dyadic relationship between you and *each* of your followers.

LMX theorists would group your friend-turned-subordinate, or others you may know fairly well and have a good working relationship with, as part of your "in-group." They would call these "high-quality relationships." You like, respect, and trust each other. It's natural to give more to these people: more time, energy, resources, support, encouragement, responsibility, guidance, information, autonomy, and trust, as well as greater input in decisions. In return, they will go above and beyond for you.

But you also manage people with whom you may not be as close—your "out-group"—according to LMX theorists. They clock in, do their job, and clock out. You don't "click" with them, and they are not very compatible with you. These are "low-quality relationships," without the same level of liking, respect, and trust that you have with your in-group. You probably don't go out of your way to include or involve them at work. And they don't go out of their way for you either.

So what should you do? Flip your script and build high-quality relationships with as many of your subordinates as possible. Research exposes the benefits. Using data from 164 studies, Charlotte Gerstner and David Day[4] conclude that when leaders have high-quality relationships, positive work experiences follow. Specifically, employees in high-quality relationships with their boss tend to have higher job performance, job satisfaction, commitment to the organization, and higher satisfaction with their leader.

The bosses everyone wants to work for are aware of the type of relationships they have with all their direct reports, staff, and team members, regardless of BFF status.

**Be fair.** As a new leader, you may believe that you should treat all your subordinates similarly and expect them to act in kind. But we know life isn't like that. New leaders (and many well-seasoned ones too) often treat some followers differently than others. And that's okay, so long as you follow these words of wisdom similar to what basketball coach John Wooden, football coach Paul "Bear" Bryant, and others have said:

*"Treat everyone fairly, not equally."*

Contrary to what you might believe, treating everyone equally isn't mandatory. You don't have to give each and every subordinate you have the same amount of equal time. You don't have to give equal bonuses or raises for every individual on your team. In fact, research indicates that treating everyone in a group the exact same way may be as dysfunctional as treating a few selected people especially well.[5]

But you should be fair. Leave the personal biases behind when allocating time, bonuses, raises, promotions, support, and resources. Many employees don't like to see preferential treatment toward a select few. The bosses everyone wants to work for don't make that mistake. They know that favoritism damages team relationships.

If you develop higher-quality relationships with some employees and not others, base those relationships on merit, not blatant favoritism. If some are provided opportunities to grow and expand in their roles and responsibilities, and if they receive development, support, encouragement, and rewards *based on their performance*, then different levels of treatment actually represent your fairness. If your former "bestie" deserved rewards and resources based on merit, great. If by something else, then gossip and distrust will follow, along with decreasing your team's morale and performance. The boss everyone wants to work for is transparent—people know exactly where they stand. Such bosses give rewards and recognition not just to their friends, but to people who perform well and deserve it. These bosses know the difference between fairness and equality.

**Be prepared.**   Steve Nowicki often portrays relationships in a four-stage life cycle: choice–beginning–deepening–ending. When you go from BFF to boss, the friendship as you and your BFF knew it has ended. It's over. Done. You and your friend must choose whether a new relationship begins. If you or your friend can't adjust, be prepared to move on. But don't burn bridges. You never know who may be leading you one day.

A person in my own Wolf Pack at work once told me, "Relationships last for a reason, a season, or a lifetime." (Funny, a girl once told me that, too, just before she stopped dating me.) My own personal torment aside, relationships change. Evaluate whether a friendship was for a reason, a season, or a lifetime. Friends can be valuable to your success and even your sanity at work. Being clear, aware, fair, and prepared will help you flip your relationships with your BFFs when they begin to report to you.

## Leading Teams

That BFF-to-boss flip is not the only reality check you'll get. The fact that your attention is less on yourself and more on those you lead and serve is a different reality for many new leaders. And believe me, focusing on relationships with your staff or team is much more difficult than just focusing on yourself. But that's what you do when you flip your script.

### Why You Should Flip Your Relationships with Your Team

When I train new leaders I always tell them, *"Two things describe effective leaders: they get the job done and they are really good at relationships."* The research behind those two claims is well established. As early as the 1940s, studies originating from the University of Michigan and the Ohio State University concluded that leadership can be divided into two types of behaviors: task- and relationship-oriented behaviors.

With task-oriented behaviors, you lead others doing the work. You drive results, helping others be productive and complete work efficiently and effectively. You'll learn more about this important flip in the next chapter.

Relationship-oriented behaviors are all the things leaders do to make others feel comfortable. It's not just about being friendly. Flip your script by understanding the importance of the relationships you have with your team.

Professors Timothy Judge, Ronald Piccolo, and Remus Ilies[6] reviewed 130 studies examining these two behaviors. Their results exposed strong relationships between task-oriented behaviors and relationship-oriented behaviors, and outcomes like satisfaction in a leader, job satisfaction, motivation, job performance, and leader effectiveness. In short, if you lead others doing the work and build relationships with them, good things happen.

Many new leaders struggle with leading teams. In fact, leading team achievement was the third-biggest challenge of new leaders in my study, mentioned by 43.4 percent of them. As described in Chapter 3, leading team achievement is also one of the four major skill gaps of new leaders. New leaders often have difficulty building teams, enhancing team chemistry, providing guidance, and communicating clear directions, goals, and expectations. They may fall short in monitoring their team's work to stay organized and meet deadlines. And they don't have the skills necessary to build and lead teams, like this man working in the energy sector:

*[My biggest challenge is] having to deal with a diverse group of people, getting the entire team going in the same direction.*

There are several reasons why managers derail in their careers, and this challenge helps explain why. According to CCL's research,[7] derailed managers tend to act like "lone wolves," working in isolation. They are described as cold, arrogant, and aloof. These failed managers often show signs of *problems with interpersonal relationships and difficulty building and leading teams.* Most people don't want to work for these types of bosses. If you don't flip your script by flipping these relationships, you may be thought of in the same way.

## What You Can Do to Flip Your Relationships When Leading Teams

You know the old saying, "There is no *I* in *team*." But there is a *me*, right?

Joking aside, teams can accomplish more than any one person. A team can bring multiple perspectives to a problem. A team can generate more information and knowledge on a topic than any one individual can. More times than not, teams come up with more accurate, creative, and higher-quality solutions than any one person can.

As a new leader, you are expected to lead teams to greater performance, which is something not many individual contributors are known for, recognized for, or expected to do. Teams expert Dr. Eduardo Salas has coauthored over 320 journal articles and book chapters and coedited over 20 books, mainly on teams, teamwork, and designing and implementing team training strategies. He and his colleagues have studied teams in government settings, armed forces, law enforcement—even in spaceflight and operating rooms. In one of his investigations, he and his colleagues examined 50 studies that linked leadership and team effectiveness.[8] They noticed that task- and relationship-oriented behaviors were tied to three important outcomes: (1) how productive teams are; (2) how effective team members believe the team to be; and (3) team learning (whether teams seek feedback and continuous improvement, discuss errors, and revise processes).

As a new leader, you clearly lead others doing the work (I'll go deeper into this in the next chapter). But what Salas and his colleagues found even more critical was that focusing on relationships contributed more to explaining team outcomes than attending to the tasks of the team. As a new leader, work to enhance relationships and cohesion among team members; motivate others; and build camaraderie, trust, and respect. When you are the boss, you can make or break your team's effectiveness, performance, and ability to learn not just by leading them in doing the work, but especially through building your relationships with team members.

So here's the one big takeaway that will help you flip your script by flipping your relationships with teams: DAC.

## Direction, Alignment, and Commitment (DAC)

When the subject of teams comes up when I train new leaders, I tell them to think about the best bosses they have ever worked for. Go ahead and do the same. Would you say things similar to what coworkers of the new leaders I studied mentioned?

> *His ability to promote a vision and strategy stands out. . . .*
> *She inspires others to move toward a common vision and*
> *shared goals. . . . She works hard to ensure that her team*
> *members feel empowered so they can deliver their best*
> *work. . . . He recognizes the strengths of his team members*
> *and uses that for the overall good.*

Like these examples, when people describe what their bosses have done to lead teams, those descriptions fit nicely into a three-part model Cindy McCauley, Bill Drath, and their colleagues offer.[9] They have noticed that anytime you have a collective of people with shared work, such as the teams you lead, you know that leadership is happening when you see three outcomes: direction, alignment, and commitment (DAC).

**Direction.** Each and every person on your team should agree with what the team is trying to achieve and that the goal is worthwhile. You've painted the picture so well that everyone agrees what success will look like. If people on your team have varying opinions on what success is or what the end goal is, and they feel like they are going in multiple directions, you don't have direction.

**Alignment.** Each person knows his or her roles and responsibilities and what others are doing. Each person knows what a "meets expectations" level of performance is and what "excellent" performance means. If people in your group start to feel isolated and don't know what is happening, and have varying opinions about what excellent performance is, you don't have alignment.

**Commitment.** Each person should be dedicated to the work and committed to the team. The success of the team, more than any individual praise, is the top priority. Team members want what is best for the team. It is your responsibility to check in with your team, both individually and as a collective. If people are more self-interested than team-focused, then you don't have commitment.

When I train new leaders, I tell them it is their responsibility to establish direction, shape alignment, and sustain commitment with their teams. The bosses everyone wants to work for do those three things really well when they lead teams.

## FOSTER THE RELATIONSHIPS YOUR TEAM MEMBERS HAVE AMONG EACH OTHER

When you establish direction, shape alignment, and sustain commitment within your teams, you help your team feel engaged, secure, and safe in the work. Recently, Google's People Operations[10] discovered that psychological safety—feeling safe to take risks and be vulnerable with each other—is the most important dynamic that describes effective teams. According to Professor Amy Edmondson and her colleagues,[11] research on psychological safety, studied since the 1960s, has shown that it's critical for people to voice their opinions, concerns, and solutions, and is linked to teamwork and learning.

As I mentioned in Chapter 1 with Brené Brown, vulnerability is an important aspect of work. Team members may feel stupid or embarrassed if they don't know the answers to a problem, or they may fear ridicule if they fail at a risky venture. So, it's important that your team members feel safe, that they can take risks and feel vulnerable with each other. To be the boss everyone wants to work for, flip your script by encouraging team members to ask clarifying questions if they don't know the answer. From the very start, assure them it's okay to take on new roles, try things out, and that, in most cases, making mistakes won't be the end of the world.

## The Platinum Rule of Motivation

Remember the platinum rule discussed in Chapter 3? The bosses everyone wants to work for tend to follow this rule when it comes to motivating others: Motivate others the way they want to be motivated.

As they establish direction, shape alignment, and sustain commitment, many new leaders struggle with how to motivate their direct reports and teams: over 25 percent of new leaders in my research said motivating others was one of their biggest challenges. If you can take people who may not be all that into work and motivate them to do their work and be their best, you have developed a bond and improved performance. Anytime you do this, it's to your advantage.

**FOUR DIFFERENT TYPES OF MOTIVATION**

According to Edward Deci and Richard Ryan[12] and their self-determination theory, there are four types of motivation:

- **External**—driven by external rewards (like money or promotions) or the threat of punishment (like not wanting a demotion or not being fired).

- **Introjected**—driven by a desire to maintain a personal sense of self-worth and avoidance of guilt or anxiety because of failing to do something that "should" have been done.

- **Identified**—driven by work that allows a person to fulfill values and goals that are personally important or may help address an important problem (like improving the environment).

- **Intrinsic**—driven by a person's own innate interests, doing something because it is enjoyable or fascinating.

As a new leader, it's your responsibility to know these four motivations and understand which one (or ones) primarily motivate each of the people you lead and serve.

What makes motivating others tricky? You can't just focus on one motive, particularly money, rewards, or praise. Granted, there are a lot of people who believe in external motivation—the more money you give, the more praise you heap, the more motivated a person will be to do their job. And both laboratory and field research by Chip Heath[13] corroborates that thought pretty well: many of us are biased to think that extrinsic motivation is the way to motivate people. No doubt, people value money, and studies that date back to the 1960s show financial incentives are related to performance quantity.[14]

But as Dan Pink suggests in his book *Drive*,[15] although money, rewards, praise and punishment are acceptable in the short-run for simple things, they simply won't motivate people to do complex work for the long haul. Other research suggests those of us who are more externally motivated by pay or compensation are, in fact, less satisfied as employees, have a strong desire to leave our organizations,[16] and are less productive and committed to our work activities.[17] Money, compensation, incentives—they just aren't the long-term answer to motivate people.

You probably don't have the resources or control to give raises, bonuses, and promotions to everyone you manage either. Plus, not everyone shows up to work just to collect a paycheck. As Jeffrey Pfeffer said,[18] people will work for money, but what they want more is to work to find meaning in their lives, to believe they and their work matter, and to have fun too. That's their motivation.

To make motivation more complicated, everyone has a different "motivational profile" based on different levels of extrinsic, introjected, identified, and intrinsic motivations. I was on a research team, led by Professor Laura Graves,[19] that examined these profiles among 321 leaders. Those with the highest job satisfaction, organizational commitment, and lowest intention to leave their organizations had some motivational similarities. They were driven by their personal values, goals, and interests, and in pursuing work that is personally interesting, important, or enjoyable. They were way less concerned with external motivations, doing things for rewards or to maintain their own self-images.

The managers with the lowest levels of job satisfaction and organizational commitment, and who had the highest intent to leave their organizations, were different. They had average levels of external motivation, which were higher than the well-below-average levels of the other three types of motivation.

It's not about dollars, or euros, or yen. Instead of thinking exclusively of rewards, pay, or compensation, understand what drives and motivates each person you lead. Flip your script when it comes to motivation—it's not some blanket method that covers everyone. Motivate others according to each individual's need. The bosses everyone wants to work for understand what motivates each of the people reporting to them.

## My Own Attempt at Flipping My Relationships

To close out this chapter, here's my own not-so-successful attempt at flipping my relationships. Here's what happened with a big data leadership (BDL) project I inherited when I became a leader.

*When I took over BDL, I didn't know much about how it began, where it currently stood, where it needed to go, or the importance of it. And the people—I knew nothing about the team dynamics and who did what. I didn't fully understand why BDL was so important to our division. I didn't really know what motivated people to do their work and why they were passionate about being part of the project, if they even were to begin with.*

*In my first meeting, the former project leader handed over the position of "team lead" to me, and she was going to stay on as a member. All I really did in that first meeting was say hi, let people say where the project was and what they were doing currently on the project, and go over timelines of what needed to be done. That was pretty much it.*

*One thing I wish I had done? Provide direction. I should have been more assertive at that first meeting, let people know my vision of the project, how important it was, and why. I wished I had conveyed how BDL can bring in revenue, add value to our work, and fuel our passions. I didn't, and I think it hurt my efforts going forward.*

*As time went on, people were not as responsive with deadlines and timelines as I'd hoped. They lacked alignment. They needed someone to hold them accountable. More importantly, they needed someone to constantly tell them what their roles were and how important their work was to bring the project to completion. That's what a leader does, and I didn't do it very well.*

*They also didn't see me as a leader who was wholeheartedly behind the project. So, they lacked commitment— if I wasn't committed to it, they wouldn't be either. What probably made matters worse, I never really took the time to meet with each of the team members individually. In my mind, I thought that if I did that, I would be seen as a "micromanager." But what I should have done was to talk*

*to each of them and find out what motivated them, what
fueled their passion for the work, and then matched their
motivations and passions to the work that needed to be
completed.*

A few months later, I told my boss and VP that the goals set
for BDL would not be met at the end of the year. It was embarrassing and painful to admit that I could not lead this team
effectively. I felt like a failure. And that was on me. Clearly, you
can see that (1) nobody knew the vision or goals to achieve;
(2) nobody knew what the tasks were and how those tasks
were important in achieving those goals; and (3) nobody was
engaged or motivated to do the work. No DAC.

But my boss and VP helped me see this as a learning opportunity. "So what will you do differently going forward?"
they asked me.

*I will help paint a picture of why BDL is so important for
each of the members of the team. I'll have weekly meetings
where members will keep themselves updated on what is
going on, so they feel connected and have clarity about
what is happening. It's a way for team members to publi-
cally say how they are fulfilling their work and be held
accountable. If someone isn't doing the work, we need to
help that person understand how that negatively affects
everyone. Finally, I will talk with each of the team members and understand his or her own personal motivations
and passions. I'll use that information to keep each person
motivated and committed to the work.*

Let the lessons I learned from BDL help you flip your script
by flipping your relationships. It's not too late. Provide DAC

and get to know others, their passion, and what drives them and motivates them.

But for me, that wasn't the only thing BDL helped me realize.

The work still has to get done. What happens if it doesn't? As a new leader, do you just pick up the pieces and do it all yourself? Read the next chapter and find out.

**THE COACH'S CORNER—YOU CAN FLIP YOUR RELATIONSHIPS**

Go to the companion website and visit the resource page for this chapter to find ways to shrink your out-group and grow your in-group, build and enhance relationships with your team, work with people across different generations, and discover the one word that may strengthen your ability to flip your script by flipping your relationships.

Here, find two questions and two applications to help you flip your relationships.

**Question 1: Do you strive for equality or fairness?** Think about your definition of being fair. What is it? How is it seen right now in managing your direct reports, staff, or team?

**Question 2: How are you flipping your relationships with your team?** What have you done recently to show your direct reports, staff, or team that you have taken an interest in them? How have you tried to understand each of their needs?

**Application 1: Make DAC clear.** In your next meeting with your entire staff, team, or all of your direct reports, use the last 15 minutes to set direction, alignment, and commitment.

*Direction*—Verbalize your message so that everyone is clear on the collective aim, mission, vision, or goal.

*Alignment*—Draw a direct line of sight between the tasks and roles each person plays and the overall goals of the team.

*Commitment*—Stress the importance of each person giving their entire effort to do their job and accomplish team goals.

**Application 2: Understand what motivates others.** Over the next 30 days, find out what motivates each of your direct reports, each person on your staff or team. Have you recently observed what each person likes and doesn't like about his or her job? That will give you a clue. If you don't know what really motivates your direct reports, have a conversation with them. Ask why each person wants to work at your organization and what exactly he or she wants to get out of work.

Flip your script by flipping your relationships. You can provide DAC and foster, maintain, and enhance the work and dedication of the individuals and teams you lead and serve, no matter their age, job title, or experience.

## chapter 5

# Flip Your "Do-It-All" Attitude

*BDL is not going to meet the year-end goal. But what can we do going forward to get the product out and back on track?*

*Okay, let's delay the rollout a month. Wait—what? The user's guide needs more work? Training protocol needs approval? Marketing needs to be notified? Sales sheet needs a revision? Decisions on pricing aren't vetted yet? Internal communications needs more information? IT needs to be in the know?*

*There's no way we can do all this in a month now. How is all this work going to be completed? How can I complete all of this?*

If you've felt like I did with BDL, an identity crisis creeps in (or has gone full blown). For me, it was running stats, analytics, and writing reports and articles. For you, it can be any number of things that made you special and unique as an individual contributor. Making the most sales. Fixing things right the first time. Providing the best customer service. Writing the best story. Creating the best pitch or design. Being the force behind a patent or product. In the script of individual contributors, that's how work is defined.

But as a new leader, your work is different. The work you once did won't earn you recognition and won't make you a successful leader. So if it's not about doing all the work, what do you do? What's your script?

Well, it's probably *not* like the one had by these new leaders who have struggled with flipping their "do-it-all" attitude. Read how their team members feel about them:

> *He struggles delegating work. He's obviously busy, and we are looking for work to do. I feel he doesn't trust us to do the work. . . . She needs to delegate more, even if it takes a little longer to finish the work. Eventually, her team will have greater capacity to do great work if she can transition more tasks to her team . . . Delegate to staff and challenge staff to "stretch" themselves . . . He needs to find his way as a leader to drive and lead his team to deliver, in the same way he himself delivers . . . Use her technical expertise and extensive knowledge about the organization to coach other scientists and technicians and help them grow.*

So what do you do?

First, you don't do all the work anymore. Second, you develop others.

## You Doing Your Team's Work Does Not Make the Dream Work

To be the boss everyone wants to work for, *you don't do all the work anymore.* Now, it's your responsibility to ensure the work of your direct reports, staff, and team is actually getting done—and that you are not the one doing it all (or taking credit for it). Lead others to accomplish goals, get the work done, and be productive. One part of flipping your script is flipping your "do-it-all" attitude.

## Why You Should Flip Your "Do-It-All" Attitude with Your Team

Many new leaders become confused about work. They believe they must develop both managerial and personal effectiveness. This confusion ranks second among the biggest challenges new leaders face. Nearly 43 percent of the new leaders in my research find it difficult (or nearly impossible) to balance being a great employee and a great boss at the same time.

Some new leaders feel they must do the work because there is not enough time or resources to get the work done. But many others do the work because they know it better than everyone else. They may feel or flat out say:

*The work that you do just doesn't measure up. I can do it so much better, so much faster, and way more efficiently and effectively than you can. Just let me do it. It's easier that way, and I know it will get done.*

What are you really telling others when you don't let go of the work? When I ask new leaders this question, here are some common answers:

- "I don't trust you."
- "My way is better."
- "I don't think the work will get done if you do it."
- "You are not good at your job."

- "When you don't do the work the way I need it completed, it will make me look bad."

Many new leaders get into trouble because they often struggle with letting go of the exact thing that made them successful. CCL calls this inability "too narrow of a functional orientation." It consistently shows up as the biggest problem area leaders have in derailment. Technical skill and knowledge are valuable for individual contributors. But this strength as an individual contributor becomes a weakness in your new leadership role. Your ability to do all the work, no matter how good you are at it, will not compensate for the inability to lead others doing the work. If you don't flip your script, you are on the track to derailment. That should be reason enough for you to flip your "do-it-all" attitude!

New leaders who flip their script realize that enhancing their relevant leadership skills and job-specific skills isn't meant to separate themselves from the pack. "It's not about me anymore." Rather, it's to simplify and accelerate the ability of their direct reports, team, or staff to accomplish their work. Flip your "do-it-all" attitude, and continue to be productive and drive results as a leader of others. Flip from "me" doing the work to now driving results and providing role clarity so that "we" as a team can do the work and be successful.

## What You Can Do to Flip Your "Do-It-All" Attitude with Your Team

You don't do it all by yourself—"It's not about me anymore." Flip your script. According to teams expert Dr. Eduardo

Salas and his colleagues,[1] team members should have all the information they need at their fingertips to get the job done and know all the procedures necessary to get the work accomplished. When you flip your "do-it-all" attitude, you drive results and productivity by leading others to perform the work, and you reduce ambiguity and provide structure to the work. According to Salas, the inability to do this is the biggest team killer! As he says, let your team know "who does what, when, why, and with whom."[2]

Now, there may be times when you roll up your sleeves and work alongside your team members. The bosses everyone wants to work for would. But they also know this doesn't occur all the time, not even the majority of the time. And it's not about doing the work at the expense of, instead of, or in spite of all the members of your team. When you flip your "do-it-all" attitude, you are still results driven, focusing on the task and productivity. But it's your team, not you, that demands your attention. Flip your "do-it-all" attitude, and drive results and productivity by leading others doing the work, not by doing it all yourself.

One other thing you do when you flip your "do-it-all" attitude is delegate. To be the boss everyone wants to work for, you clearly don't do the work. However, you also don't necessarily give people the work you hate doing. The boss everyone wants to work for appropriately and effectively delegates work. You should give someone important work and more responsibility while providing authority, resources, and support. And by delegating effectively, you free up your time to do other work that may need more of your attention. You also build trust among the people you delegate work to and provide autonomy. In the end, more work actually gets done.

If you don't learn how to delegate, your career as a leader may be shorter than you intended.

## Developing Others Is Like a Gift

An important and oftentimes neglected part of flipping your "do-it-all" attitude is something not many individual contributors are known for: you develop others. The people you lead want to know that someone—you in particular—prioritizes their development and growth. So, make learning and development a priority for the people you lead and serve. Developing others is one of the biggest skill gaps of new leaders (something that is highly important for new leaders to do, yet not many are skilled at it) and rare for new leaders to excel at from the start. Yet the boss everyone wants to work for is known for making time to develop others and believing that developing others is a top priority. It's like I tell all new leaders: developing others is like a gift, as good to give as it is to receive.

### Why You Should Flip Your "Do-It-All" Attitude by Developing Others

Of the nearly 300 new leaders I studied, more than 20 percent acknowledged that developing others is one of their biggest challenges. Tammy Allen, Lillian Eby, and their colleagues examined 43 studies that connected the act of developing others with important outcomes.[3] They discovered that those who receive development usually attain higher salaries, compensation, promotions, and recognition. If you've been lucky enough to receive development, you've probably felt such positive outcomes. Now, think of how successful your direct reports and followers will be if you develop them or support efforts to develop them! Flip your script because "It's not about me anymore." Put your attention on developing others.

---

**DEVELOPING OTHERS ALSO MAKES YOU SUCCESSFUL**

Even though you know "It's not about me anymore," you may have this lingering thought: "Developing others takes a lot of time. So what's in it for me? If I develop others, will it help me?"

Yes. Developing others actually helps you and your own career. Researchers Aarti Ramaswami and George Dreher[4] have several theoretical reasons why, which include learning more information to make you effective in your job, freeing up your time to accomplish other work, and growing your reputation. As Rajashi Ghosh and Thomas Reio concluded in their research, if you develop others, you'll tend to have higher job satisfaction and organizational commitment, and you'll view your own career as successful.[5] In my own work with Todd Weber and Golnaz Sadri, managers who were better at developing others were seen as better performers in their job.[6] And though that positive relationship was found among 30,365 managers from 33 different countries in our study, in some countries (like the United States, Canada, Mexico, Venezuela, Brazil, Argentina, Portugal, and the Philippines) that positive relationship was even stronger. In another study of 1,623 managers, John Sosik and I found that those managers who were better at developing others tended to be perceived as more promotable by their bosses and peers.[7] The science shows that developing others helps you too.

The quicker you realize developing others is part of flipping your "do-it-all" attitude, the better off you'll be, like this new leader coming to that realization:

> *I remember one day thinking to myself, "Developing others takes so much time out of my day and takes me away from my work. It's almost impossible for me to do my work anymore." Then it hit me. Developing others is my work. From that point on, I had a clear sense of what my work was all about.*

The evidence clearly shows, developing others is like a gift: it's as good to give as it is to receive.

## What You Can Do To Flip Your "Do-It-All" Attitude by Developing Others

When you flip your script by flipping your "do-it-all" attitude, you develop others to be their best. So what does the script of a boss who develops others look like? Probably a combination of what several new leaders said:

> *Passionately care about your team members, how they perform, how they could improve, how they could be promoted, how they could be seen throughout the organization and not be left behind. . . . Look out for your team members, and do what you can to give them challenging assignments. . . . Identify and bring out an individual's brightest potential, the cause and origin of one's weaknesses or struggles, and help that person overcome them.*

The boss everyone wants to work for coaches and mentors his or her staff, team, and direct reports. When you develop others, your attention is squarely on others, championing their efforts to grow, develop, and succeed. To best do that, to be the boss everyone wants to work for, flip your script by flipping your "do-it-all" attitude, and do these three things to develop others: (1) support others; (2) create goals; and (3) give feedback.

**WHAT'S THE DIFFERENCE BETWEEN COACHING AND MENTORING?**

Many people think coaching and mentoring are interchangeable. They are *not* the same thing.[8]

Coaching is building another's capacity to be effective in his or her current job or preparing someone for a short-term change or increase in responsibility. Your conversations revolve around tasks, behaviors, short-to-intermediate-term results and goals, actionable learning, and a results orientation. You provide feedback on tasks and performance. It's not, "I would have done it this way." Instead, open up a dialogue by asking, "What else could you do?" or "What haven't you considered?"

Mentoring is different. Granted, "mentor" may bring to your mind an older person helping a newbie out. It's like Obi Wan Kenobi and Yoda with Luke Skywalker in the *Star Wars* franchise or Professor Dumbledore and Harry Potter. In the "real world," it's Lorne Michaels and Tina Fey, or Tony Bennett and Lady Gaga. But being a "gray-haired old fart" is not mandatory to mentor others. Mentoring has a long-term focus with a spotlight on the person's career path and future success. As a mentor, leverage your own position in your organization and your own expertise to sponsor others and transfer your knowledge to them. You can do that, no matter how old or young you or the person you are developing is.

Success is no longer defined by all the things "I" can do. Now, success as a new leader is defined by all the things your direct reports, staff, and team can accomplish. And for them to accomplish great things, you need to flip your script: support them, give them goals to accomplish, and regularly tell them whether they are on the right track and performing well or not.

**Support others the right way.** Kathy Kram has pioneered research on developmental relationships, particularly through mentoring. She believes[9] (and dozens of studies affirm) that there are two different types of support you should provide when you develop others.

One is career-related support. You help others understand organizational life, gain exposure, and obtain promotions. Four ways to provide this type of support are listed here:

1. Build the reputation of the people you are developing by bragging about them. This doesn't take away anything from you or how you are perceived as a good employee or boss. There is no competition here (and there shouldn't be). You tell others (particularly higher management) about all the great work of the people you are developing, and possibly help those you develop obtain lateral or up-ward job opportunities. It's okay to brag about the work of others.

2. Help others develop their skill sets. Assign the people you are developing important tasks and responsibilities. Help them learn how to do the work, and provide clear instructions about how to do it (without you actually doing it). This builds their skill set. Also, give them knowledge

and understanding of the world of work. Provide advice, share ideas, and offer different perspectives.

3. Protect others from things they don't need to know. Many of the people you are developing may not know the pros and cons of getting involved in certain projects. It's your job to shield them from harm, from unnecessary risk, or from getting involved in things that waste their time.

4. Give them interesting, challenging assignments. The only way people are challenged is if they actually take on a challenge. So, give the people you are developing a difficult yet attainable task to accomplish (and if it's a high-profile task, that's even better).

The second type of support you should provide is emotional support. Those you develop often find great support from you that inevitably increases or builds up their competence, identity, self-worth, and effectiveness. Two ways to provide this type of support are by (1) being a role model and (2) accepting others for who they are. First, as a role model, you set an example for how to act and work. The people you develop will identify with you and exhibit your attitudes, values, and behavior. Second, by accepting people for who they are, you are giving support, trust, encouragement, and respect. These actions help others take risks and develop their own professional identity.

**Create goals the right way.** Simply put, goals should be (1) specific, (2) difficult, (3) yet attainable, according to researchers Ed Locke and Gary Latham.[10]

An example of being specific is to "increase the profitability of your group by 20 percent in the next six months," not to "try your best sometime soon to do something impactful."

Besides specificity, make sure the goal is difficult yet attainable. If it's too easy, people may become bored or see accomplishing it as worthless. If it's unattainable, they may give up altogether.

According to Locke and Latham, specific, difficult, yet attainable goals are linked to reduced absenteeism, fewer injuries, and increased production. Further, in 99 out of 110 studies they examined, specific, difficult, yet attainable goals led to better performance than easy, "try your best" type goals or having no goals at all. That's a 90 percent success rate. The next time you set those yearly goals with your direct reports, staff, or team, make it your goal to help others create goals the right way! See? It's not so hard to make specific, difficult, yet attainable goals, is it?

**Give feedback the right way.** Give regular feedback to the individuals on your staff and team. From this point forward, it's not about "me" and how "I" am doing; instead, flip your attention toward developing others by providing feedback.

When I introduce the concept of feedback to new leaders I train, I tell them feedback is a gift too. And sometimes, like gifts, we want to return them immediately (like that ugly pair of socks or useless kitchenware). Too often, feedback is treated the same way.

We all know receiving feedback can be awkward or painful at times; there can be a lot of emotions and feelings involved. Delivering it can be just as awkward and painful. But providing positive and negative feedback to your direct reports, staff, or team is the only way they will know how they are performing well or, if they are not, how they can become better. It's what the boss everyone wants to work for does and is part of your script now.

Giving feedback and holding people accountable is a challenge to nearly 25 percent of new leaders according to my research. If you're in that group, I recommend you adopt CCL's model of feedback. It's very simple, direct, and helps you avoid common missteps in providing feedback, such as judging individuals, not actions; being vague; or giving unwanted advice. The model is an easy-to-remember abbreviation. SBI: situation, behavior, impact. Here's how to deliver feedback the SBI way.

***Step 1: Situation.*** Describe the situation. Be specific about what day, what time, where, and when the behavior happened that you are giving feedback for.

- **Good example:** *"Monday morning at the 11 o'clock meeting in room 210."* Why is this a good example? It clearly states the place and time you are referencing so both you and the person you're giving feedback to can clearly remember the context.
- **Poor example:** *"Last week at the meeting."* Why is this a poor example? It's vague. There are many meetings that happened last week. What meeting? What day last week? What time? It's entirely possible that you are thinking of a completely different day and time than the other person is. There will be confusion from the start.

***Step 2: Behavior.*** Describe the observable behavior you are giving feedback for. It's actually what was said or what was done, something a video camera could pick up or hear. No values given. No judgments made. Simply state the fact of what was said or done.

- **Good example:** *"You spoke at the same time the presenter was going over the budget."* Why is this a good example? You focus on the behavior, the action, the facts. Because behaviors can change, you can help the person start, stop, or continue that specific behavior.
- **Poor example:** *"You were rude."* Why is this a poor example? "Rude" is not a behavior. It is a judgment. It's your impression or interpretation of what went on. Can you imagine how you would take hearing that? Probably not well. Neither would anybody else who heard that!

***Step 3: Impact.*** Describe how you felt or how the behavior impacted you, either positively or negatively. You can use positive words that reinforce the behavior, like "happy," or "proud," or "impressed." If you intend to give negative feedback encouraging someone to stop or change a behavior, you could use words like "troubled," "worried," "disengaged," or "irritated."

- **Good example:** *"I felt embarrassed."* Why is this a good example? You focus on how you felt about the behavior, the true feelings that you experienced, and *not* how it affected others. Because a person cannot dismiss what you truly felt, the feedback recipient will be more likely to hear what you said.
- **Poor example:** *"What's wrong with you? Why aren't you more respectful?"* Why is this a poor example? You didn't let the other person know how you felt. And you are likely to put

the other person on the defensive by asking what he or she was thinking or by putting your own values on what the person should be doing. You judged this individual and made him or her feel like you know what's right and wrong. Don't play armchair or Monday morning quarterback. Don't be Sigmund Freud by psychoanalyzing what is going on.

See the difference between SBI feedback and feedback without the SBI formula? Would you rather hear this?

*Monday morning at the 11 o'clock meeting in room 210, you spoke at the same time the presenter was going over the budget. I felt embarrassed.*

Or this?

*Last week at the meeting, you were rude. What's wrong with you? Why aren't you more respectful?*

You probably know the answer. So would the boss everyone wants to work for.

If you want to be the boss everyone wants to work for, and you genuinely want to flip your script by flipping your "do-it-all' attitude, feedback is essential. So if feedback truly is a gift, here are two research-based tips to help you give "gifts" that no one will ever want to return.

***Tip 1: Provide "wise feedback."*** "I'm giving you these comments because I have very high expectations, and I know that you can reach them."[11] Those 19 words may work wonders for you in giving feedback. David Yeager and his colleagues

## FLIP YOUR "DO-IT-ALL" ATTITUDE WITH PERFORMANCE REVIEWS

Performance reviews are now part of your work too. Be clear about what your organization and the HR department requires you to do; understand directions, responsibilities, timelines, and how to make and rate goals and measure behavioral change.

But if you think reviews are a ritual, just something to do to "check the box" or something that "legal" or "compliance" says you must do "or else," the person you are reviewing won't take it seriously. In what they call "perceived system knowledge," psychologist Paul Levy and his colleagues believe when employees understand the system surrounding performance reviews and know the reviews are taken seriously, great things happen. Specifically, they'll have similar ratings as yours (so that's less fussing and nit-picking); they'll have better job attitudes (always a plus); and they'll feel that the system is "theirs," and not something handed down by you or HR (so they'll feel empowered and have ownership of something).[12] So, take performance reviews seriously, and your direct reports will too. Plus, if someone is not performing up to standards, and eventually a "we-need-to-let-you-go" conversation is needed, documenting performance and taking it seriously from the start will give the evidence needed for those personnel decisions.

And finally, remember this: although an annual formality at many organizations, performance reviews are not something you do once a year. If the year-end performance review is the first time you talk about goals since you set them, it's too late to develop them. At every single meeting you have with your direct reports or individual staff members, you should review what they are doing to accomplish their goals. Give feedback often so they won't be surprised when the year-end performance review comes.

instructed teachers to provide somewhat harsh, critical feed-back (or as they suggested, "substantive and rigorous criti-cism") on papers written by their students. Some students received those 19 words (the "wise feedback"), while others didn't. Students who received the "wise feedback" were more likely to turn in a revised paper and make the suggested changes based on the feedback, and the quality of the revision was better than the original. Those 19 words (or something like them) provide a standard of excellence you hold, and they convey your belief in others. Those words can give you powerful reassurance that delivering tough feedback won't necessarily break the people you lead.

*Tip 2: Deliver feedback often.*  Many new leaders ask me how often they should give feedback. I say, "As often as pos-sible, and strive to give five positive pieces of feedback over a period of time before you must deliver a negative one." The 5:1 ratio of positive to negative feedback doesn't come out of thin air. Consider relationship experts John and Julie Gott-man and their work investigating successful marriages and those ending in divorce.[13] During conversations around con-flict resolution, the ratio of positive to negative interactions for successful couples is usually around 5:1. For unstable marriages, the ratio's usually 0.8:1. Granted, your spouse or partner probably isn't your direct report at work (unless you're part of a family-run business). But as a rule of thumb, if a 5:1 ratio accurately predicts successful marriages 80 percent of the time (and in some cases, the Gottmans' success rate is at 94 percent), how can it hurt to follow the same ratio for giving feedback?

Great bosses give harsh feedback too. But that feedback is meant to help, not to belittle or embarrass. And they give more pieces of positive than negative feedback. To be the boss everyone wants to work for, give both positive and negative feedback in at least a 5:1 ratio to the people you lead and serve.

## Keep Doing It All and See What Happens

This chapter should give you some great evidence and reasons why you can't do all the work anymore. But let's say you just can't let it go. Think about what happens if you don't flip your script by flipping your "do-it-all" attitude. Picture it.

> *Your coworkers have all gone home. You are still at work, doing their work. You are probably regretting it too.*
>
> *Your team hasn't accomplished anything major recently. If you asked them, probably none of them know what to do, when to do it, or why.*
>
> *You see it in their faces. They are disengaged. They don't feel supported.*
>
> *And they feel stuck in their jobs. They aren't able to grow as people, develop as future leaders. They don't have goals, and they rarely get feedback on what they are doing to better themselves.*

Do you want these people working for you?

It doesn't have to be this way. You can flip your script. Realize that as a new leader you can't do it all anymore, nor are you supposed to. You now help others understand what their work is, drive their results, and develop them by providing support, goals, and feedback.

But it's not just about the work either. As you flip your script, you'll come to find out that the work becomes much broader than before. You interact with other groups and work across the organization, seeing politics at play. So you must flip your perspective, the subject of the next chapter.

---

**THE COACH'S CORNER—YOU CAN FLIP YOUR "DO-IT-ALL" ATTITUDE**

On the companion website, the resources page for this chapter gives you certain questions you can ask when you have coaching conversations, tips on how to make your staff or team meetings more enjoyable (or at least, tolerable), as well as ways to deal with conflict among your team.

Here are two questions and two applications to help you flip your "do-it-all" attitude.

**Question 1: What is delegation for you?** Think about all the positive things that can happen when you effectively delegate work. How are you developing others by delegating work to them? How can your work become easier when you effectively delegate work to others?

**Question 2: How are you flipping your "do-it-all" attitude with your team?** What have you done recently to make sure the people you lead and serve are doing their work, and doing it well? How are you simplifying and accelerating the ability of others to achieve goals and objectives? How are you clarifying processes, roles, and responsibilities? Organizing, scheduling, and providing structure to their work?

**Application 1: Brag on the accomplishments of each of your direct reports in the next one-on-one meeting with your boss.** Write out one thing each of the people who report to you is doing effectively and the positive impact that this is having on you, your staff, team, and/or organization. Share those with your boss. Don't have a meeting scheduled with your boss for a while? Schedule one and make it happen in the next two weeks.

**Application 2: Give five positive SBIs to each of your direct reports, staff, and team members over the next 30 days.** It may sound daunting, but you can do it. If you aren't experienced at giving feedback, if it's not a natural part of your script, start by writing it out. Next, practice saying it in front of a mirror. Then, in your next formal one-on-one meeting, deliver it. Don't have a meeting scheduled for a while? Proactively see or call the person this week and deliver the positive feedback. The more frequently you are able to give feedback, the easier it will be.

## chapter 6

# Flip Your Perspective

*So, I've made it to "the inner sanctum"—my first manage-
ment team meeting. I always wondered what it was like in
here. Before, my friends and I only speculated about what
went on in these meetings. Now, I get to see what it's
really like.*

*It's nothing like what we thought.*

*I've only been here for five minutes, and I'm in way
over my head. All the managers are talking about lack of
resources, needing more people. And a lot of their suggestions
sound like they are at my expense. Are they trying to steal
some of my people? Steal some of my budget? It's my first
meeting for goodness sakes.*

*I need to stop this. I must talk about my group and what
I need. That's how things get done around here, right? But
that sounds so selfish. How do I do that so I don't piss other
people off? That's not the impression I wanted to leave in my
very first management team meeting. Does it have to be "I
win and you lose?"*

*Later in the agenda, we will discuss a long-term strategy
for our entire department. How do we communicate better*

*to the entire organization and effectively work across boundaries to show how important our group and department are?*

*Who am I to say? I just got here!*

*I'm out of my league. What am I supposed to do?*

## Being Politically Savvy Is Not a Bad Reputation to Have

My first management team meeting was something I'd much rather forget than remember. I was the newbie. All the other managers had been managing their groups for years and had way more experience. One was actually my boss years ago. I felt like I didn't belong. It showed.

They talked about their teams, which after a few weeks in my new role, I felt I could do too. But they also discussed resources, stakeholders, strategy. They each had a desire to portray how their specific team was an integral part of the organization. I had a completely new team and no clue how we fit in with the strategy of our department or our organization, or how we work with different stakeholders to bring value across the organization. These were all examples of the type of perspective that was considerably different, bigger, and unlike anything I've ever had to think about before. It can be unnerving for any new leader.

In this chapter, you learn what that meeting made all too clear to me. I had to flip my perspective. You do too. Most individual contributors have a narrow view of what goes on in their organizations. Now that you're a new leader, flip your perspective. What does that mean? See things more broadly. Expand your vantage point. And realize that politics exists!

If you don't flip your script by flipping your perspective, and account for the politics in your organization, what will people say about you? Things similar to what was said about these new leaders:

> *He needs to broaden and increase his degree of influence over projects and people (including those he does not formally manage) by developing win–win solutions. He needs to think a couple of steps ahead, and gain buy-in from stakeholders. . . . He should become more active in the broader corporate community so he can better understand the needs and perspectives of colleagues in other areas, especially those senior to him. Then, he can meet their needs and better influence decisions across the organization. . . . He doesn't build consensus outside of his group to move larger ideas forward. . . . The internal relationships of this organization are not what she is used to. She has years of service but is considered an outsider to some of the management staff. Not fostering personal relations with peers has really worked against her.*

As you flip your script by flipping your perspective and you start to take on that bigger view, you'll quickly see the organizational politics at play. Your ability to flip your perspective has a bearing on how well you manage politics, how well you work with coworkers and stakeholders (up and down as well as across the organization), how you feel about your organization, and how well you do your job. Crummy politics have grave consequences, but embracing that perspective is not your only choice. You can flip your perspective, prosper in your organization, and be the boss everyone wants to work for.

## Why You Should Flip Your Perspective

Many new leaders have a certain perspective on politics, for example, fulfilling their own agenda or working on projects personally satisfying to them. They want resources just for themselves at the expense of others. They are blind or closed-minded when it comes to understanding how others feel, how others can be helped, or how to share resources. For many new leaders, that win–lose mentality is there from the start. Why? It's that old breakup line again, "It's not you; it's me." They must win, or refuse to lose, because frankly that's all they have ever known. It may even be the way they see their own leaders act.

For many, politics is a necessary evil or a game to play. Favoritism, bullying, power struggles, and self-interest abound. These individuals see people making others feel small, stealing credit, or passing off the work of others as their own to get attention, glory, power, or resources. And bending or blatantly breaking rules and manipulating the system or people to get what they personally want. It's Frank Underwood in *House of Cards*.

Many new leaders don't like seeing things this way and feel bad for succumbing to this view of organizational politics. They see politics as an unfortunate reality that can't be avoided. It's very discouraging, often demoralizing. They can't comprehend how this perspective can be flipped. Just look at the word *politics*:

*Poli*—from the Latin, meaning "many."

*Tics*—a bunch of blood-sucking insects.

That's taken from Gerald Ferris and Pamela Perrewé, who have been studying politics for more than three decades. Their research[1] portrays a grim picture. If you only see people going along to get ahead, cutting corners to get what they want, being rewarded for behaviors not formally endorsed by the organization, forming cliques to gain personal power, and/or the "favorites" being rewarded with higher pay and promotions, you'll sense that the environment is rather threatening and unpredictable. You'll feel less in control and won't understand what should and shouldn't be rewarded. The ambiguity can be confusing, upsetting, maybe even debilitating as Perrewé and her colleagues' research shows; when politics is viewed in this manner:

- The health of workers is negatively affected.
- Conflict, stress, strain, tension, fatigue, and anxiety all increase.
- Feelings of helplessness, victimization, and burnout all increase.
- Performance at work is negatively affected.
- People want to leave their organizations.[2]

For one-third of the new leaders I studied in my research, managing internal stakeholders and politics was a current challenge. Of all the challenges, it ranked fourth. Consider the words of a woman in the nonprofit sector, who said:

> [There is a] new focus on quality and speed, but peers are resistant. They find comfort in the old way of doing things. Unlike my peers, the new focus on quality and speed excites me, and I want to move faster than those around me. This causes friction, and I don't know how to

*acknowledge their concerns and yet still get them to move faster.*

Or this woman in the financial services sector, stuck with managing up:

*My first line supervisor and second line supervisor have two very different (often opposing) leadership styles. One is "full speed ahead," and the other is "proceed with caution." The challenge is managing messages to both of them, since they often have opposing views. My first line supervisor may direct work; the second line disagrees with the direction. It's a difficult place.*

Unfortunately, managing politics won't go away, and you will continually face it as you progress in your career. I once led a study[3] asking 763 leaders from China, Hong Kong, Egypt, India, Singapore, Spain, the United Kingdom, and the United States the following question: "What are the three most critical leadership challenges you are currently facing?" These were all well-seasoned leaders with years of management experience, mostly in middle to upper middle or executive levels of management all over the world. They clearly knew how to lead others. Yet, struggling with managing internal stakeholders and politics was as relevant a challenge for them as it is for new leaders.

Organizational politics will not go away. You may not like to deal with politics. You may despise it, may even feel trapped by it and feel there's just no other way but to act like everyone else.

No one blames you for feeling that way. But there is an alternative.

Flip your perspective.

Those who flip their perspective see politics differently. This is not to say that they are naïve. They understand that there are competing interests, scarce resources, ambiguity, unclear rules and regulations, and a lack of information. They see it all.

The difference? They don't let those perceptions get in the way of their goal to bring transparency and clarity to their teams, their coworkers, or stakeholders they work with. They remove uncertainty in the environment.

When you flip your perspective, you no longer cut corners, play favorites, or work the system to get things for yourself at the expense of others. You don't perpetuate the self-serving behaviors and ambiguity that fill organizations. "I have to be right all the time" is not part of your vocabulary.

Politics is not a game to be played, where you have to win and everyone else loses. In fact, it's not negative or positive. Politics is simply the air we breathe in organizations. When you flip your perspective in this way, you'll survive—even thrive—at navigating politics in your organization with your political savvy, and feel good about yourself and the way you do it too.

You are not stuck with just one view of politics. When you flip your perspective and see politics differently, you'll do what the boss everyone wants to work with would do: remove uncertainty and bring transparency, clarity, and a shared meaning to those you work with, so everyone knows what to expect by using your political savvy.

Ferris and his colleagues describe political savvy[4] in ways I also see in my research and training of new leaders.[5]

- Understand yourself and the environment around you.
- Use that knowledge to be flexible and versatile enough to obtain goals that benefit you and others.
- Act in a sincere and authentic way.

That doesn't sound bad, does it? Being politically savvy does not mean someone else must lose for you to win. It's not about selfishness, having a façade, being a chameleon, or inauthenticity. Instead, it involves the sincere use of your skills, behaviors, and qualities to remove uncertainty and obtain goals that benefit you and others at the same time.

Being politically savvy is a must in modern organizations and in fact relates to many positive consequences. Across 130 studies, Ferris and others[6] found that politically savvy people tend to

- feel more satisfied with their job;
- experience more commitment to their organization;
- be more productive with their work;
- go above and beyond what is outlined with their work; and
- have better career success and prospects for their future.

My own research shows the benefits of political savvy. Over the years, we continuously find that managers with political savvy are seen as better leaders, more promotable, and less likely to derail in their careers according to their boss, peers, and direct reports.[7] So don't think of political savvy as being a brownnoser, a backstabber, a backroom dealer, a schmoozer, a shark, or a snake. It's not embarrassing, patronizing, or inauthentic. And it's not being part of the "old boys network" either; Jean Leslie and I have found that women rate themselves just as high in political savvy as men do, and the positive relationship between political savvy and performance is the same for both men and women.[8] There are no meaningful gender differences.

Having political savvy is a good quality that benefits you, your coworkers, and stakeholders in your organization. So, flip your perspective.

## What You Can Do to Flip Your Perspective

Here's the skinny: *Understand what you want, what others want, and determine where there is common ground so everyone wins and benefits.* To do that, you need political savvy. According to Ferris and his colleagues, and my own work and research, there are four different aspects of political savvy that you can develop.

**1. Read the situation.**  Objectively scan, observe, and gather information about yourself and the people and the environment around you. Academics call this "social astuteness." You are highly self-aware with your own thoughts and behaviors. You also thoroughly understand the thoughts, behaviors, and needs of coworkers and stakeholders you interact with.

**2. Determine the appropriate behavior before acting.** Based on observations of what is going on around them, politically savvy bosses learn what to do in a given situation. Find common ground and do what needs to be done, so everyone wins something and feels good about the final result. You don't manipulate others to get what you want. Instead, work through the system to ensure everyone's needs are served.

Determining the appropriate behavior also means you don't come unglued in times of crisis either. You don't lose your cool. It's about impulse control and remaining calm in the storm that is around you. It's thinking before you speak and act.

Many of us have told an inappropriate joke, shared information publicly that should have been kept private, acted without a care in the world, or became a volcano when mistakes were made. Some of us realized later we shouldn't have done those things; we lived to tell about it and learned from our mistakes. Others, however, are no longer around because of that lack of impulse control and inability to think before speaking. They lacked political savvy. It's the type of thing many people don't come back from. Truthfully, it almost set back my own career. Here's that story.

*I was in the middle of training a leadership development program at CCL. A high-ranking official, whom I knew rather well and considered just as much a friend as a superior in my organization, needed a status update on a project, inquired about my schedule for an upcoming meeting, and asked if I could be part of that meeting's agenda. So, during a break I quickly wrote an email saying I was currently in a program training about 25 leaders, could only attend a portion of the meeting next week, and that I couldn't put anything together given the short notice. To close the email, I wrote down a couple of problems our project encountered.*

*I thought I was being attentive to her needs. For me, it was less about the content of the email and how it was worded, and more about the action of sending an email*

*quickly to show that I was attentive to her needs of wanting
information.*

*The way my superior read that email was much different.
A couple of weeks later, she gave me feedback on what she
read. The two major lessons I learned:*

*1. The email was blunt, terse, and discourteous. I needed
to layer some context around the email. I was in a program
but should have let the reader know I'd give what I could
now and would provide more detail later.*

*2. Second, I gave problems, not possible solutions. In the
leadership role I have, I can't just say what's wrong. I need
to broaden my perspective; identify concerns and come up
with possible solutions.*

*Looking back, I should have taken a little more time and
not have been so abrupt. Moreover, I needed to flip my
perspective. If I give problems, I should offer solutions too.
Or given the context (not having enough time to give a
detailed email because I was in the middle of training a
program), I should have said that we could talk about
coming up with solutions later.*

We all have probably made a mistake of not thinking before speaking and have acted on an impulse. But you can avoid
it with your political savvy.

**3. Network strategically.** This is not about having the most
friends on Facebook, the most connections on LinkedIn, or
the most followers on Twitter (by the way, follow me on Twitter
@Lead_Better). It's not about going to conferences, joining
social, professional, or civic groups and collecting a stack of
business cards. Networking strategically is building strategic

relationships and garnering support for your goals and those of your coworkers and stakeholders. By connecting with influential individuals who hold different resources and valuable assets, you'll gain a voice where you might not have been heard otherwise. More importantly, you could gain access to important information from key insiders.

So what does a strategic network look like? ODD: open, diverse, and deep. Through their research, that's how Phil Willburn and Kristin Cullen-Lester at CCL[9] describe the networks of successful leaders.

> *Open*—The people you know in your network should not all know each other (that's a closed network). When you have an open network, the people you know are connected with other people that you don't know. With this open network, you'll likely hear new information you never would have before, gather different ideas and perspectives, and capitalize on that information to influence others or make well-informed decisions that benefit all parties involved.
>
> *Diverse*—Those in your network should not all be from the same group or division (that's a homogeneous network). In a diverse network, the people in your network should be from different groups and divisions and should cross several different boundaries, including up, down, and across the formal hierarchy, as well as those that span functional or geographic boundaries. When your network can span these boundaries, you can build bridges so that all involved feel part of the solution.
>
> *Deep*—What you know about the people in your network isn't just their name, title, and where they sit (that's a shallow

network). It goes deeper than that. Knowing where they went to school, what team they root for on the weekends, what their pet's name is, or what their kid did to win the talent show is a good start. But it goes deeper still. Get to know these people: understand what they do, the situations they are in, and their motives, values, and needs.

**4. Leave people with a good impression.** Many of us who study political savvy believe what Ferris suggests: if you have political savvy, you appear not to have it. Everything you do—your behaviors, your actions, the words you say—are all genuine, transparent, and authentic. As a boss with political

---

**ANYONE CAN NETWORK STRATEGICALLY**

Now, some of us love networking. It energizes us. Others find networking a chore, painful and draining. Your feelings aside, networking strategically is necessary, and anybody can do it.[10] If the thought of building an ODD network makes you nervous or anxious, take it piece by piece. Networks aren't built over a weekend, so be patient. To help ease your apprehension, remember: it's not about having the most connections. Look beyond the formal organizational hierarchy and org chart, and be strategic about who is in your network. It will be worth the time and effort in the end because these ODD networks can give you a foundation upon which to exchange information, resources, and skills. You'll gain the perspective and resources to garner support and build camaraderie in the workplace for things you and others need now and in the future. It's the type of thing the boss everyone wants to work for would do.

savvy, be sincere and authentic in all that you say and do, and leave people with a good impression.

Think about the politically savvy attributes. If you read the situation in a sincere and authentic way, you will be described as "astute" or "ingenious" or "clever." But if you do it in an inauthentic way, you'll probably be labeled as "cunning" or "sly" by others. Determine your appropriate behavior in a sincere and authentic way, and you'll be seen as "flexible" and "adaptable." If not, you may be regarded as "cold" and "calculated" or possibly "Machiavellian" in nature. Network strategically in a sincere and authentic way, and you are a "relationship builder," but if not, you're branded a "brownnoser" and "power hungry." Which adjectives would you want attached to you?

Think about leaders without political savvy, those who haven't flipped their script. You know those people. They are seen as manipulative and selfish. They are like snakes in the grass (or maybe snakes on a plane, for Samuel L. Jackson fans). They say one thing, shake your hand, and stab you in the back later.

Do you want to manipulate someone to do something? Probably not. Even thinking about that probably feels disingenuous. But do you wish to sincerely and authentically influence someone to get what you and others need? That's when you know you've flipped your script by flipping your perspective. Leave people with a good impression by being sincere, trustworthy, and genuine. You'll build trust and confidence with those you work with now and in the future.

For some of us, this may be difficult. Maybe you've gotten some feedback that people see you as self-serving and manipulative. Maybe you're afraid there's just no other way. Well, fear no more. Ferris, Perrewé, and their colleagues believe that although political savvy is somewhat innate, it can be trained, developed, and enhanced in new and experienced leaders alike. I believe it too, as I continually help new leaders become aware of political savvy and, in programs and workshops, help them develop it.

Make it a point to flip your perspective. You can do it! It's not how to manipulate people to achieve an outcome. Flip it. Choose to behave genuinely, and exhibit sincerity and trustworthiness to reach a goal all parties want. You have the potential to be considered a well-respected, politically savvy boss in your organization.

## Two Ways to Flip Your Perspective

Up to this point, you've read how important it is to flip your script, shining the spotlight less on yourself and more on the people you lead and serve: "It's not about me anymore." As you flip your script by flipping your perspective, shine the spotlight in many different directions to many different stakeholders inside and outside the organization. As you do, your political savvy will help you deal with two of the topics I frequently hear about when I work with and train new leaders: "How do I manage up?" and "How do I manage in a matrix?"

**Manage up.** For many, "managing up" leaves a bad taste in their mouths. They think of it as self-promotion, kissing ass, brownnosing, pandering, bowing down, sucking up, not leaning in, or selling out. When you flip your script, you see it differently.

First, don't think of it as managing your boss, superiors, and the like. Think of it as helping your senior colleagues. Managing your boss sounds like you are trying to get your boss under control. Helping your senior colleagues is less formal and stuffy, shows respect, and sounds less manipulating.

Second, think of helping your senior colleagues as part of your job. Take responsibility of the relationship and be proactive. It's your job to seek out, understand, and influence your senior colleagues, not their job to find you, tell you what they think, and agree with what you want. If you have political savvy, you inform your senior colleagues about what is going on. You keep them in the loop. You're busy, and so are your senior colleagues. So, be proactive in keeping your senior colleagues informed because they can't know everything happening with your team.

It's not brownnosing. Think of it this way: if you were in their shoes, what should they know about you and your team? That's keeping your senior colleagues informed. They'll be able to communicate that information up and across the organization.

**A WARNING WHEN WHAT GOES UP DOESN'T COME DOWN**

Words of caution: Don't get sidetracked in making "managing up" 100 percent of your job. Remember the derailment research: careers go off track if you neglect your team. So, spend the appropriate time helping your senior colleagues help themselves and leading your own direct reports, staff, and team.

**The Matrix is not just a movie.**  Quick story:

> *About two months into my role as director, I was in a*
> *difficult situation. I have an employee who reports to me,*
> *but the person isn't in headquarters and frequently must*
> *respond to the needs of that location. So, I'm a boss who*
> *doesn't have complete authority over the person. It's very*
> *hard to get the person focused on work because many times*
> *this individual doesn't know what to do and asks, "Should I*
> *focus on what you tell me or what the people in my location*
> *tell me?" And because role clarity is so important in leading*
> *teams, I knew I needed to give that to my direct report. But*
> *how, given the reporting relationship?*
>
>   *I went to my VP for help. Her response?*
>   *"Welcome to the matrix."*

Contemporary organizations are more complex than the
hierarchies that structured them in the past. Some of our reporting relationships are in the matrix—we report to our department and a functional manager. Matrixed relationships
are hard to manage. But not impossible. Find what makes your
stakeholders tick. Listen to what they're telling you. Find the
common ground. This is how I dealt with the situation:

> *My direct report, my boss, my VP, and a senior colleague*
> *from the location in which my direct report works, all had a*
> *conference call.*
>
>   *It was 10:00 P.M. my time, an hour in, and I was*
> *struggling, frustrated, and sleepy. All I heard was "Do you*
> *realize what we are up against?" and "Do you know the*
> *things we are trying to do?"*
>
>   *By listening to the pressure points and needs of my senior*
> *colleagues, I found the common ground that would help*

*everyone on the call. On the spot, I said something directed
to the senior colleague at the other location.*

*"I truly sympathize with all that is occurring. I have a
better understanding of the work you are doing and understand you are targeting a certain population. So, how can
we in research help you with your strategy? Can we think of
ways to do our research and target the population you feel is
most important to you and your business?*

My VP IM'd me immediately and gave me a great vote of
confidence, saying, "Great reframe." That's when I knew I'd
done something cool. Around 10:45 P.M. my time, it felt like
everybody had won. To be clear, I have no direct authority
over my senior colleagues (just the opposite). But because I
expanded my perspective and looked at things through their
eyes, my political savvy enabled me, from my less senior position, to align our work to the other location. And my direct
report feels more engaged in the work. Everyone wins.

## Coming Full Circle

I have come a long way since that first management team
meeting. Granted, I sometimes feel like an imposter in those
meetings. But I am growing more comfortable in my role. In
fact, I remember the exact moment I felt like I sort of be-
longed. My mindchatter before the meeting went something
like this:

*Another team meeting, the usual suspects—don't look like
an idiot! Actually, you won't. You'll do great.*

*First thing on the agenda, we are talking about develop-
ment planning of those working in our department. You*

*will make sure to speak up for the people that report to you. Plus, show how increasing their effectiveness can directly help the other groups in our department too. This will show you genuinely care not just for your people, but for your peers and their people as well.*

*Second on the agenda is our own team development. From our own internal opinion surveys, we on the management team know that we are falling short in some areas. People don't feel connected to each other. Ask your peers how we together can get our people to feel more connected. They have been in the organization and in their management role longer than you. So what have they seen or heard in the past that has been effective in getting people to feel more connected?*

*Final item on the agenda: How can our groups get better at internal messaging, at making clear to our stakeholders across the organization what we do and why it's important. So try to understand our stakeholders' point of view. How is our work important to them to get their work done? What would they need from us that could help right now?*

Later that evening, I went out to a business dinner with some of my peers from that meeting. Upon leaving the restaurant, two of my peers praised the way I handled myself in that morning's meeting. I asked them for clarity and feedback, what exactly it was that I did. Each told me I expanded my perspective. I also thought of things from their own perspective and from our stakeholders' perspective too. That kind of thinking was needed in our group.

I truly felt like I flipped my perspective. I was looking out for my team, working well with my peers, and helping my senior colleagues. Without my political savvy, none of that would have been possible.

I felt great driving home that night, just like I did when I first got my promotion months ago.

Then a rhetorical question hit me:

*Why did you flip your perspective? In fact, why did you flip your mindset, skill set, relationships, your "do-it-all" attitude—any of it? Do you truly have a desire to help the people that report to you? Do you really want your colleagues to succeed? Or are you doing these things for your own personal gain?*

Like me, you have a choice to make. Will you lead from your own personal agenda? Does it matter what you do, so long as the ends justify the means, or the means justify the ends? Or will you be aware at all times that your actions and decisions can affect others, whether you know it or not?

Flipping your focus is the final act, probably the toughest in flipping your script. It's the one that takes the most amount of soul searching. One with the highest stakes that can affect more than just you and the people you lead and serve. It may sound ominous, but it can be addressed, as you'll read in the next chapter.

**THE COACH'S CORNER—YOU CAN FLIP YOUR PERSPECTIVE**

If you are interested in finding out other ways to flip your perspective by enhancing your political savvy and helping your senior colleagues help themselves, go to the companion website and the resources page for this chapter.

Here, you will find two questions and two applications to flip your perspective.

**Question 1: What does the politically savvy person in your organization look like?** Think about the person in your organization who has a lot of political savvy—the one who reads the situation, knows what to do, has a strong network, and is truly genuine in everything he or she does. What are concrete examples of the way that leader used political savvy to bring transparency to the workplace and to offer solutions so everyone wins?

**Question 2: What is the perspective of your senior colleagues?** What are your senior colleagues' pressure points? Their pains or anxieties? Their needs? What are their agendas, values, goals, and missions? If you can answer these questions, you can better understand what you and your team can offer to make their jobs easier and make them successful.

**Application 1: Show your senior colleagues one way that you have the ability to help them meet their needs over the next 30 days.** Think about your own strengths and what you or your group can bring to fill a need or over-come inadequacies, deficiencies, or limitations, given the rules and realities of the workplace. Then, suggest how you or your team can help fill the gap. Or talk with your peers about their strengths and determine how to address those gaps together.

**Application 2: Map your network.** It's like your own "Six Degrees of Separation with Kevin Bacon" game, but you are at the center.

1. Start with a blank sheet of paper.
2. Write your name in the middle, and draw a circle around it.
3. Think of the many people you are connected to:
   - The people you know really well
   - Those who you don't know well, but would like to

- The people who you work with closely on a daily basis
- The people who you work with, but who are out on the fringe
- The people who you ought to know in the future as you progress in the organization
- The people who you know have a lot of power and influence
- Others important to you

4. Put the names of those people with whom you have a strong, high-quality relationship (like those described in Chapter 4) close to you on your map.

5. Draw circles around those names, and connect your encircled name to theirs.

6. Put the names of those you have a weak or distant relationship with farther from you.

7. Draw circles around those names, and connect your encircled name to theirs.

8. Notice that distance means something in this map. Not everyone in your network map will have a line of the same length.

9. Connect your connections. If one of your connections has a deep relationship with another one of your connections, connect those two names together with a line. Do the same for all connections you feel have deep connections with each other.

On page 140 is an example of what a network map could look like. Now that you've made your network map, see if your network is in fact ODD. Is it open? Is it diverse? Is it deep? If it is, what can you do in the future to ensure your map stays that way as you progress in the organization? If it is not ODD, ask if some of your close connections can help you connect with those more distant, or maybe more strategic.

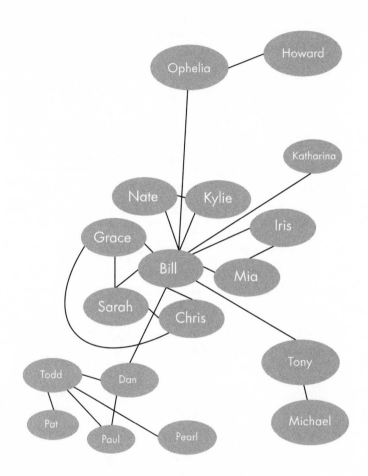

An example of a network map.

## chapter 7

# Flip Your Focus

*You've had some really tough decisions to make. Some pretty small. But there are other decisions that are a little more complicated and distressing. Should you cut that project's budget over another project? Do you give that piece of feedback to someone even though you know it will be hard for the person to hear? Do you really have to officially reprimand someone or do you let it slide? Do you recommend going forward with a decision that is cost-effective even though some cuts are involved? It's so uncomfortable. But there's this quote from a CEO:*

> *"You will be confronted with questions every day that test your morals. The questions will get tougher, and the consequences will become more severe. Think carefully, and for your sake, do the right thing, not the easy thing."*

I love that quote for a couple of reasons. Whether you are an individual contributor, a brand-new boss, or well-seasoned leader, it speaks to where your focus is. Where is your integrity? Your character? How do those come into play when you make decisions? The quote speaks to the difficulty of doing what is right. It's difficult to do, and even when we try, we may fall short. Mistakes will be made in our careers because we are imperfect people. But what I hope you realize, now that you are a leader, is that your actions and decisions, and the aftermath, may be amplified. It's not just you who may deal with the consequences; your actions and decisions will affect others too. As a new leader, own it. Now that you are a boss, your focus must constantly be on your character, integrity, and doing what is "right." Why?

Let's face it: people look up to leaders and expect a lot out of them, damn near close to perfection 24/7/365, at work and even away from work. You may even feel the same about your leaders too. I know I do. On the flip side (pun intended), you probably have people right now looking up to you, expecting just as much. That's a hard thing for any of us to live up to. The pressure can be unbearable at times, I know. I feel it myself as a new leader. I feel it's way too much to ask, and it borders on being unfair. But that's what many of us demand from our leaders. It comes with the territory of wearing the "Leader" T-shirt and "Boss" hat.

You clearly have a lot of power and influence over others. And so you have the potential to affect the lives of people outside of your own. "It's not about me anymore," remember? Accept it.

For some new leaders, that's a huge rush, and it fills them with pride. For others, it can be intimidating, maybe even a little frightening or humbling to think about. However you feel, don't take it for granted, because it's so damaging to so many when leaders are involved in scandals because they didn't flip their focus, and they didn't focus on integrity, character, and doing what is "right." Every few months, a leader's inability to flip his or her focus and realize just how much his or her actions and decisions affect others comes up in the news and blows up into some sort of scandal.

It's pretty heavy stuff, but too important not to bring up. In my opinion, flipping your focus—understanding and embracing that who you are and what you do can have repercussions beyond yourself—is the most challenging aspect of flipping your script as a new leader.

## Oh, the Irony

There's another reason why I love that opening quote. Picture yourself on your graduation day. Your commencement speaker, a CEO of a multibillion-dollar global organization, motivated you with those words of advice. Then, you throw your cap in the air and get your diploma, ready to take on the world.

Two weeks later, that same CEO, who gave such an amazing speech and inspired you so much with that quote, is arrested.

That's what happened to former Tyco International CEO Dennis Kozlowski.[1] At a commencement speech at Saint Anselm College, he spoke those words to the graduates. Seventeen days later, he was arrested and later was found guilty of grand larceny and conspiracy, falsifying business records, violating general business law, and misappropriating (or stealing) hundreds of millions of dollars from his organization.

Why do I really love this quote? Irony. A leader, talking about morals and doing not what is easy, but what is right, didn't follow his own advice. He only looked out for himself and didn't care how his actions and decisions would affect others. He didn't flip his focus. The quote constantly reminds me that even though I am human and imperfect, if I don't flip my focus, I am no better than Kozlowski. It could happen to me.

So, would you do the "right" thing in every situation, in the face of difficulty, unpopularity, discomfort, and distress? It's easy to say, "Of course," when it's just a hypothetical or a scenario on paper. I know I would. Anyone would. No-brainer. But if our lives as leaders resemble anything like the TV shows with hidden cameras or the latest gossip news on TMZ, people don't always do what's right. Many are self-centered, only think of the short-term gain, and don't always think of how their actions affect others and the future. They still believe, "It's not you; it's me." They never flipped their focus.

We are all human. None of us are perfect. But I will level with you. You know as well as I do, people look up to you, put their trust in you, follow your example, even emulate you because you are their leader. You will make many decisions in your career. Your actions and decisions will affect others whether you know it, realize it, are purposefully doing it, or not. This chapter will help you understand just how important flipping your focus is now as a new leader, and for the rest of your career.

Some, though, may feel this chapter comes a little too late. You, or others around you, may have already started to question your actions and decisions as a new leader. Maybe things you did before your promotion led to these rumblings. Be assured, it's not too late to change course. Use this chapter to check yourself so you don't ultimately wreck yourself. Get the proper insight, the tools, and the confidence from this chapter to flip your focus and be the boss everyone wants to work for.

## Why You Should Flip Your Focus

Although I hope my passion about this topic convinces you of the importance of flipping your focus, I know that some of you may still be skeptical. I get it. You see that others get promotions, fame, and fortune without ever thinking about the implications of their decisions. I've had similar thoughts too. But don't allow those thoughts to convince you to not flip your focus. Here's why.

**Character and integrity at the top.** When you flip your focus, you understand that your actions and decisions affect more than just you. All leaders have agendas. Some are very self-focused (what philosophers would call ethical egoism). Many of us are like that; we want to make it to the top. There's nothing inherently wrong with it. But as a leader, you must seriously consider flipping your script by flipping your focus. Thinking about the greater good (what philosophers would call utilitarianism) or doing what is best for others, not yourself (i.e., altruism) will come across your mind. You'll start to question what you really should do and where your focus really should be. That's where your character, particularly your integrity, comes into play.

Starting in 2010, my colleagues and I began looking not at character flaws, but instead at the character strengths of leaders.[2] In particular, we concentrated on 4 of the 24 character strengths Christopher Peterson and Martin Seligman classified

**DEFINING INTEGRITY, BRAVERY, PERSPECTIVE, AND SOCIAL INTELLIGENCE**

- *Integrity*—Acting in accordance with your stated values, showing consistency in your words and actions, following through on promises, and using ethical considerations to guide decisions and actions.
- *Bravery*—Acting decisively to take the lead tackling difficult problems and persevering in the face of unpopularity, threat, or challenge.
- *Perspective*—Understanding the perspectives of different functional areas in the organization and having a firm grasp of external conditions affecting the organization (like business opportunities and challenges, business trends, and the strengths and weaknesses of competitors).
- *Social intelligence*—Understanding your own impact on situations and people, knowing what makes you and others tick, understanding their motives and feelings, and having the ability to adapt your behavior to what the situation dictates.

in their "Values in Action" model[3]—integrity, bravery, perspective, and social intelligence.

In our first study, we investigated these four character strengths among 191 top leaders of organizations (presidents, CEOs, and the like). The direct reports of these 191 leaders supplied the ratings of the four character strengths, and the bosses (in this case, board members) of the 191 leaders told us how effective these top leaders were in their jobs. After crunching the numbers, integrity, bravery, perspective, and social intelligence each positively related to performance. So, for example, top leaders who were high in integrity tended to have pretty high job performance ratings. And those who weren't high in integrity likely performed pretty poorly in their jobs. We found the same pattern of results for the other three character strengths too.

Looking deeper into the data, we also learned which of the four character strengths was most important. Integrity came out on top. In the highest of levels in an organization, character strengths are important to a leader's performance. And of the four we analyzed, none are more important than integrity.

Character and integrity are even tied to the financial performance and bottom lines of organizations, and how people feel about their jobs too. According to research by KRW International,[4] CEOs rated as having high character, including integrity, had a five times greater average of return on assets than CEOs with low character. They also found that employee engagement was 26 percent higher in organizations with CEOs high in integrity. Character does matter at the top, especially integrity.

**Character and integrity in the middle.** In our next study of character strengths, we examined 246 middle-level managers—the leaders to whom you more than likely directly report, where your next leadership promotion will likely take you. Same variables as before, same method, same results: integrity, bravery, perspective, and social intelligence, each positively related to performance ratings. If you want to be effective at the next level, our results recommend you need strong character.

And just like before, we dug deeper into the data to find which of the four was most important. We were surprised.

Social intelligence, not integrity, was the most important char-acter strength. And when we looked at all four character strengths together, integrity had very little to do with how well these middle-level managers performed their job.

As you know, we usually get promoted based on our current performance, not the things we need in the future. Our findings suggest that integrity is not seen as being as important to the current performance of managers working in the middle of organizations. So leaders climbing the cor-porate ladder might not necessarily have the character strengths necessary at the highest of levels. No wonder so many people think you don't need integrity to reach the top. It sort of played out in our research.

**Character and integrity for you, now, in your current role.** So now you may be left wondering,

*What about new leaders like me? The research suggests integrity may not matter as much in my next step up in the organization, but it is definitely needed at the top. But what about now? As a new leader, do I need it now, where I am in the organization?*

You may or may not be surprised by this. There was an absence of the mention of integrity in the close to 300 new leaders that I studied. For example, there were no mentions of integrity in any of their top challenges. I also collected writ-ten comments about the strengths and development needs of the new leaders from their own bosses, peers, direct reports, and new leaders themselves. In total, there were 3,294 written responses. Fascinatingly, only one entry, from a new leader's direct report, mentioned that integrity was something that the new leader needed to develop. Looking at the strengths of these new leaders, integrity was mentioned only 96 times in the 3,294 entries. That's less than 3 percent.

Why is this the case? Why does it look like integrity and character and doing what is "right" just doesn't matter all that much unless you are at the top? Well, one way to look at it is that perhaps it's just the "price of admission" to your new leader role. Perhaps integrity and character and doing what is "right" are treated as "a given" when you become a boss. That's just what we expect of our leaders. Only when people have ethical failures does it come into our consciousness. Many times, unfortunately, it's too late to do anything about it.

But you can do something about it now. Flip your script by flipping your focus. If you are interested in climbing the corporate ladder, making it to the top, and having that corner office with the windows looking out on the skyline (and don't forget that all-important access to the executive washroom), you need integrity and character. Let these studies convince you to flip your focus. If character, particularly integrity, will be even more critical to your success as you continue to progress to the top levels of your organization, why not focus on it now and be prepared for your future?

But what if you have no desire to climb the corporate ladder? You don't want to put in the time and effort to get that corner office. Being the next CEO or president of your organization is not your end goal and is not your definition of career success. That's okay—there's nothing wrong with that. But realize, that's not an excuse to not flip your focus. Your actions and decisions will carry weight, and lapses in character and integrity can catch up to you, no matter where you are in the organization. It can happen to anyone.

Now some of you may be thinking:

*Okay, I know integrity is important in flipping your focus, and that I need integrity, especially if I intend to go higher and higher in the organization. Not a problem. I have integrity.*

No doubt, many of you do have integrity, and your followers are lucky. We all know how much integrity we truly have, right? Like this famous leader said:[5]

*[I] lived my life in a certain way to make sure that I would never violate any law—certainly never any criminal laws—and always maintained that most important to me was my integrity, was my character, were my values.*

Truly, this leader thinks he has character and integrity. So who was he?

Former Enron CEO Kenneth Lay. He said this in his first primetime interview on CNN's *Larry King Live* after pleading not guilty to criminal counts. I probably don't have to tell you how many suffered from the corruption of Lay and others from Enron. Clearly, Lay overestimated his integrity.

Lay's story shows you that oftentimes we misjudge and in fact overestimate our integrity. As a matter of fact, our character strengths research[6] hints to this phenomenon too. Leaders in our study tended to overrate how much integrity they had, particularly the top-level leaders we studied. Interestingly, the new leaders I studied also tended to overrate their integrity compared to what their direct reports saw.

## The Real-Life Evidence

Although the studies speak to the importance of character strengths, particularly integrity, others still might not be convinced that they truly do matter. You've seen people make it to the top and not get caught. They reaped the benefits and got away with it. If it worked for them, it can work for you too, right?

As I wrote this chapter, Martin Shkreli (the thirty-something pharmaceutical executive who jacked up the drug Daraprim from $13.50 a pill to $750) was arrested for securities fraud and essentially running his business like a Ponzi scheme. Then there's Bernie Ebbers of WorldCom, John and Timothy Rigas of Adelphia Communications, or Bernie Madoff. They were all leaders in their field, were connected with fraud, and got caught.

How about United Airlines CEO Jeff Smisek trading perks for influence with senior officials at the Port Authority of New York and New Jersey? Or several officials from FIFA, international soccer's governing body, who received kickbacks and bribes? They got caught and personally suffered the consequences.

But their actions and decisions didn't just affect them. Failing to flip their focus affected so much more than just the individuals involved.

Think about what happened at Worldcom or Adelphia, for example. The actions and decisions of those leaders didn't just set in motion the downfall of their organizations, but also affected the livelihood and well-being of those who worked there. People lost jobs, couldn't collect paychecks, couldn't make a living, and that affected their families, their kids.

Do you think the decisions made by Volkswagen leaders who allowed the implementation of illegal software to help cars cheat pollution tests hurt only them? Look at the stock price of Volkswagen after the scandal; their stockholders and investors felt the pain in their pocketbooks, wallets, and 401(k)s. You can also imagine how the faith and trust of people who bought VW vehicles are now compromised because of it.

Many all over the world probably still lament over sub-prime mortgages and how the events surrounding decisions made at Lehman Brothers and other companies affected massive downturns in the United States and world economies. How many people lost homes, jobs, or retirement savings, or couldn't afford to care for their family or future because of those decisions and the inability of leaders to flip their focus?

Is it your plan to end up like these notorious leaders? Do you want your name even associated with those people? I would hope not. The research is clear. But it happens in real life too. Leaders do get caught when they don't flip their focus.

## What You Can Do to Flip Your Focus

You have the potential to touch the lives of so many beyond you. When you flip your focus, you understand that your impact is bigger. Your actions and decisions truly affect others. Integrity matters. And you can't just have it overnight.

**Rome and integrity.** I'm sure you've heard the old saying, "Rome wasn't built in a day." The same thing goes for integrity. Integrity takes time to develop and strengthen. Put in the time.

If you have the drive to make it to the top, you clearly need integrity. It's the most important character strength we studied. It takes time, a career, a lifetime, to build your integrity; you can't just flip a switch and overnight have it. As a new leader, start now: build your character and integrity for what is coming up in your bright future.

And though integrity isn't built in a day, it can be ruined with one action or one decision. It takes a lifetime to build your integrity, and one instance, one second, to ruin it. Always be mindful of your integrity in everything you do because one action or decision can ruin a reputation you have worked so hard to build and can affect so much more than just you.

None of us are perfect, and a lapse in character can happen to even the best of us. If it does, swallow your pride, own up to it, and work extremely hard to build that reputation of high character all over again. We all make mistakes, and it's not impossible to overcome them. But be prepared to put in the work if this sort of thing happens to you.

So the big takeaway here? Pay attention to integrity because you need it in many things you do as a new leader. In particular, you need integrity when making decisions and when building trust.

**Integrity when making decisions.** It's not easy to flip your focus. Like the quote that opened this chapter, doing what is "right" is not necessarily easy. It will test you. But the more you are able to think about it, learn about it, and prepare for it, the easier it will be to flip your focus.

If you are doing things for your own selfish interest, not understanding the ramifications of your decisions, and not caring how it will affect others, you haven't flipped your focus. The bosses everyone wants to work for, however, look beyond themselves and flip their script. How can you do that? Here are some tips to increase your odds of doing the "right" thing when the time comes.

***What would Mom or others think about you?*** Ask yourself if the behavior you are about to engage in or the decision you are going to make would be approved by your mother, grandmother, or primary school teacher. If you think that's a bit too far out there, what would your current coach or mentor think? What would your wife, husband, or partner think? Is this something you want your friends to read about in the local paper or the *Wall Street Journal*? Fifty years down the road, how would you describe what you are about to do to your grandkids? What would they think?

***Promise and then deliver.*** Be clear about what you can do and the timeframe around it. Confidently commit to what you can do. Then deliver on it. Don't "overpromise and under-deliver" as the old saying goes. A proven track record of constantly promising and then delivering builds your integrity. And proverbially speaking, when your "mouth writes checks that you can't cash," your credibility and integrity take a hit. The more that happens, the more difficult it is to recover.

***Learn from why good people do bad things.*** We tend to think that only bad people do bad things. But that's not

## YES, YOU CAN SAY "NO."

*I get that you probably intend to please those who ask for your service or help. It doesn't matter if it's your boss, your coworkers, customers, or other important stakeholders. You can't stand disappointing others or coming across as being lazy, impolite, unsympathetic, uncaring, or selfish. I feel the same way. I hate saying "no" to anybody.*

*Even though we know deep down inside there's just no way we can do everything requested of us, many of us can't say "no." And when we say "yes" and then end up not delivering on what we said we would do, it gets us in trouble. Or we actually do fulfill the request at the expense of others who depended on us, and we lose our credibility with them. The quality of work probably wasn't its best. And worse, your team may feel like they weren't heard, weren't consulted, that their input didn't matter, and they were thrown under the bus because you didn't say "no" on their behalf.*

*So what do you do? You can't say "no," right?*

*Well, yes, you can! Give yourself permission to say "no." In fact, saying "no" when you truly can't fulfill the request can be a blessing because it will set some boundaries. Of course you'd like to help—be up front with that. But be transparent about why you are saying "no," given the parameters and circumstances surrounding the request in that moment in time and what you and your team are ultimately responsible for.*

*Then it's up to you whether that "no" is the final word or whether it's the bridge to another conversation to work together to find the proper and best alternative.*

*You can still have integrity and say "no." You are telling the truth, aren't you? It's when you say "yes" and you don't deliver that your integrity takes a hit.*

necessarily the case. Researchers have shed light on the fact that good people, even us, may do bad things or may not do the "right" thing even though we know better. We oftentimes don't do the "right" thing because we don't fully comprehend the entire situation; we don't see the big picture or understand the actual choices we can make.

But you don't have to fall into that trap.

First, don't dwell on the people in the present, but rather, think about the future. Many of us like to help people, which is a noble thing to do. It's totally natural and normal to care about and help the people we like. Yet doing so can cloud our judgment and prevents us from seeing what's wrong in our actions and the future repercussions. By no means am I saying you no longer should help people or that how you feel about someone shouldn't be part of your decisions. But according to research by Lamar Pierce and Francesca Gino,[7] you shouldn't let your relationship, or wanting to help someone, be the driving force and only reason behind your decisions. They recommend taking yourself out of the situation. Understand exactly what the cost to the future will be. How will your decisions truly affect you? The other person? Other people connected to your decision? That will be difficult because we can't predict the future, and it's so much easier to deal with the people we like in the present. But that's how you can flip your focus and do the "right" thing. Fully understand the possible aftermath of your decisions, and be transparent to all parties involved about why you are making that decision.

Second, know the triggers and pressures that prompt making the wrong decision. There are circumstances or situations that would predict us acting unethically, or doing the "wrong" thing when we know all too well that we shouldn't. Bazer-man and Tenbrunsel in their book *Blindspots*[8] and dean of Harvard Business School Nitin Nohria summarized research[9] indicating we are more likely to act unethically when we work in uncertainty; we are under extreme time pressure; we work alone; or there are big rewards (usually monetary) tied to our work. If you are in any of these situations, you are more likely to go down a path you shouldn't go or make a decision you don't need to make. Act with integrity and do the "right" thing, particularly under these circumstances.

**Integrity is needed when building trust.** Although the findings of our character strengths research suggest that integrity only really matters at the top, trust is a reason why integrity is critical to you now as a new leader, and in your future, no matter where you are in your organization. Integrity has a lot to do with building trust. And as a leader, you know that without trust, you won't get things done. So how do you build trust? Apply the work of Roger Mayer and his colleagues,[10] cited over 13,000 times according to Google Scholar at the time of me writing this (so trust me—or Google, it's good).

First, understand that you don't have control over how trusting other people are. Some people are more trusting than others. So go easy on yourself if it seems difficult to build trust with someone—he or she may not be that trusting of anyone. Trust is not an automatic guarantee with everyone.

Second, to build trust, you must be trustworthy. Some people have an easier time being trusted than others. It's usually because they are trustworthy, which embodies three elements according to Mayer and his colleagues: *ability* (are you highly skilled within the domain that is relevant to the relationship); *benevolence* (do you want to do good by the other person); and—you guessed it—*integrity*. And you can't get away with just one of these; you really need all three.

Third, take a risk. If the other person is willing and you are seen as trustworthy, the next step is to take a risk and determine if the person can be trusted. Remember Brené Brown's work: a little vulnerability goes a long way. That's how trust really starts. Maybe it's giving someone a project that you have some apprehension about because the stakes are high. Maybe it's asking someone to do something a little beyond his or her talents, resources, or time. Maybe it's having that person stand in or represent you in an important meeting or by delivering an important presentation. But that's a necessary risk to take to build trust. And know that the other person is taking a risk too. If he or she does come through, that person is banking on you acknowledging it, giving him or her proper recognition, and not leaving him or her hanging out to dry. If the outcomes are favorable for both you and the other person, trust will grow. If not, trust fades.

Trust is essential to relationships at work, and there's a big prize in the end once it's built. A team of researchers led by Jason Colquitt[11] analyzed 119 different studies and observed a consistently strong connection between high levels of trust and (1) high levels of job performance, (2) high levels of going above and beyond what is required in jobs, and (3) low levels of doing things that are counterproductive to the work and productivity of organizations (like sabotage or stealing). And in their study, although ability, benevolence, and integrity (the aforementioned three indicators of trustworthiness) are needed, Colquitt and his team found integrity had the strongest relationship to trust for leaders. Flip your focus, and you can build better and more trusting relationships at work. In the end, trust will benefit you and, more importantly, the people you lead and serve.

## It's Not Easy Writing about This Either

Flipping your focus is hard. It isn't easy writing about it either. In fact, this was the hardest chapter for me to write in the entire book. I'd write something. Then rewrite it. Then change it again. And again. Over and over and over again. I felt like I could never get it right. I wanted the perfect words there on paper, to help you understand just how important flipping your focus is, because not enough is being done about it.

I also found it hard to write this chapter because I didn't want to scare you out of your mind. I didn't want you to feel that you must be perfect every single second of every single day or else you'll fail as a leader. That was not my intention.

Let me make this absolutely clear: you don't have to be perfect in everything you do, and you shouldn't feel like you can't make mistakes. You will make mistakes. I do. We all do. And most mistakes can be fixed. In fact, decades of research through our "lessons of experience" work at CCL show time and time again that we learn from our mistakes and failures, and they make us better leaders and people.[12]

There's a reason why this is the last part of your script to flip. Aside from being the hardest part of your script to flip, in my opinion it's the most important to how you lead and what your future will be as a leader. I hope as you read this chapter, you are fully aware your actions and decisions can affect the lives of not just the people you lead and serve, but your family, friends, and possibly people way beyond your control or span of influence, now and in the future. You have the ability to be a great leader, one that people look up to and follow, one that is a shining example of character, integrity, and doing the "right" thing. Flip your focus and be the type of boss everyone wants to work for, not just for the rest of your career at work, but just as importantly, in your life away from work with your family, community, your place of worship, and the society we all live in.

---

**THE COACH'S CORNER—YOU CAN FLIP YOUR FOCUS**

If you go to the companion website and the resources page for this chapter, you will find other ways to think about the importance of your integrity and character in everything you do, ways to enhance your character, ways to think about doing what is "right" when making decisions, and certain things to mention when you have to say "no" to people.

What follows are two questions and two applications to help you flip your focus.

**Question 1: Why did leaders have lapses in integrity and ethical failures?** Do some research on a person with an ethical failure. What started the person down that road? What choices did the person have? What did the person do or not do? How can you make sure the same won't happen to you?

**Question 2: How should you display trust?** Think about the leader in your organization who has the reputation of being trustworthy. What does she or he do to enhance that reputation?

**Application 1: Do a self-assessment.** Think about the following and honestly answer these questions:

- Do I walk the talk? Are my actions and words consistent?
- Do I take a stand on things that mean a lot to me, my values, and principles? Am I true to myself?
- Am I able to say what must be said when the situation demands it? Can I speak about the tough issues?

**Application 2: Have a reality check with your own integrity.** It is difficult for many of us to take the time and understand how we see ourselves and our character. And it's just as difficult getting feedback on our character too. In the next 30 days, ask your coworkers the same questions about your integrity as you asked yourself in Application 1. Use an anonymous survey. Or maybe a face-to-face conversation can help, that is, if they know what they say won't be used against them (which is a strong indicator of your integrity right there). It will be tough, maybe even extremely hard feedback to hear, particularly if you plan on asking those whom you may not get along with or have a less than ideal relationship with (and I highly suggest you do). But that's what you do when you flip your focus. Better now and not when it's too late.

## chapter 8

# Stick with Your Flipped Script

*Since becoming a boss, I've struggled with helping others realize just how important their work is. I see how valued they are to our team and organization. But I just can't quite get them to see it.*

*But today, I had the best call ever with one of my direct reports! She just completed a project and clearly sees how valuable her work is. And she had fun doing it too. Over the phone, I could hear it in her voice—how excited and proud she was of her own work. It felt like she'd turned a corner and has purpose and meaning that she never saw or felt before. She's now ready to take on more work and make new goals to stretch herself.*

*What's that secret sauce or magic formula so that can happen with everyone all the time?*

That phone call was one of the best feelings I've had as a boss. My direct report felt energized with her work. She felt her work truly mattered. Looking back, it wasn't one thing I did, but several, over a long period of time that brought her to that realization. For months I was deliberate in giving her clear direction and outlining her roles and responsibilities. We had several coaching conversations about her current work, and mentoring conversations about her future aspirations. At times it was exhausting and frustrating for me and probably for her too.

And in that one 15-minute phone call, all of that work was worth it. Everything came together for her. Granted, it's not always like that in every phone call after that one, and there are times it feels like I have to start all over. I still make mistakes in my capacity as a boss. But at least I know it's possible for someone to feel engaged at work, like they and their work matter. And that I had a hand in it. What an awesome feeling.

## The Secret Sauce

That secret sauce, that magic formula? Sticking with your flipped script, the script of the boss everyone wants to work for, and not reverting back to the "It's not you; it's me," script.

Psychologist Robert Eisenberger would likely approve. Arguably best known for his "organizational support theory,"[1] he believes that if we feel our organization cares for us, we "pay back" the organization through our efforts, increased performance and commitment, and by going above and beyond our jobs to help our colleagues and our organization reach goals. The theory holds up as one of the most well-established explanations of employee–organization relationships and why employees do what they do; findings from 558 studies substantiate the theory's claims.[2]

So why is this important for you as a new leader to know and understand?

Although employees form opinions about support from their organization, Eisenberger believes they form general beliefs about how much their leaders—that's you—value their contributions and care about their well-being.[3] As a leader, you represent, symbolize, and personify the organization to your direct reports. So those who report to you attribute how well the organization supports them based on how well you support them. Shine the spotlight on others. "It's not about me anymore."

Some may be hesitant about that.

*She is a rock star. She gets everything done. She reminds me of me. And in many cases, she's a lot more talented than me, even with a lot more potential. She gets all the credit, accolades, recognition, and opportunities that I used to get when I was an individual contributor not so long ago. Hate to say it, but I'm a little jealous. She may steal my job one day. How is that going to look?*

Yes, you may get defensive and insecure. You may even start to think of ways to "undermine the underlings." It happens to all of us. But those are from the "It's not you; it's me," script. If you have truly flipped your script, you know that "It's not about me anymore," and your job is to shine the spotlight on others. You'll be satisfied and happy with the success of those you lead and serve. You'll want what is best for them.

If the people you lead and serve are successful, you are successful. Think about it. Maybe you are leading a small team right now. If they are successful, you'll be seen as a driver of results and developer of talent. You'll be given more responsibility. You'll lead more people. If they continue to be successful, maybe you'll lead an entire department, division, or function one day. The success of those you lead and serve will bring you success if you stick with your script. Don't go back to "It's not you; it's me." Realize "It's not about me anymore," and stick with that.

Other bosses definitely want to provide support and care for the well-being of those they lead and serve. But they think their whole persona must change. "Sounds like I have to start giving hugs to people," they may say. It's not about giving hugs (though, if you are known as a person who gives hugs, it's a normal part of your organization's culture, and it's welcomed by the one getting those hugs, it won't necessarily hurt). But if you give "professional hugs," things that Eisenberger and his colleagues would suggest—telling people how important they are, for example, or appreciating their efforts, listening to their concerns, asking for their opinions, giving formal and informal recognition of their achievements—then you show that you value the contribution and care about the well-being of those you lead and serve. Support, develop, and attend to the needs of your direct reports, staff, or team. Make them feel appreciated and valued. They need to know that their best interests are your top priority. And there isn't one blanket way to give professional hugs to every single person. Remember the platinum rule: make others feel appreciated and valued the way *they* want to feel it. That's sticking with the flipped script. That's what the boss everyone wants to work for would do.

### YOU DON'T HAVE TO SOLVE ALL THE PROBLEMS—JUST LISTENING MAY HELP

There are times we just want to poke our heads in the office or cube of a staff or team member and say, "Hi, how are you?" and then run along to our next meeting. Or do the same with just a quick two-minute phone call. But then you either see something is off by the person's face or nonverbals, hear something that just isn't right, or he or she just comes right out and starts unloading. Now you feel as if you are being pulled into a vortex. And you probably feel you must now fix all this person's problems.

Stop. You don't. These people are adults and don't need fixing. What they need is to feel valued and recognized. What they need is to feel like someone is in their corner, that someone has their back.

That someone is you.

If you don't have the time right at that second, be up front with it, and schedule something with that person as soon as your schedule is free. But if you do have the time, just take five to ten minutes, sit with him or her, and listen. It might not seem like all that much, and you may never get any praise for it. But that one act can make a world of difference to that one person. Even the simple act of listening is something that the boss everyone wants to work for would do for the people they lead and serve.

## Connect the Dots

The bosses everyone wants to work for instill a purpose, motivation, and meaning with every single one of the people who report to them and work with them. The people they lead and serve understand just how important and meaningful their work is to the team and organization. They understand how their lives matter. That's connecting the dots.

Part of the foundation for Adam Grant's popular work *Give and Take*[4] is his early research on generosity, motivation, and meaningful work. Through multiple experiments in the lab and in organizations, Grant exposed the power of meaningful work.[5] How did he do this? For example, in several studies,[6] Grant brought into the workplace what he calls "beneficiaries," or end users who shared their stories of how they directly benefitted from the work of a team. The results? The team's performance, sales, and revenue all increased afterward.

Obviously, when people clearly understood how they and their work mattered to others, and how their work was significant and provided meaning to others, their dedication and performance increased; they felt more satisfied in their job; and they persisted through tough times. That's connecting the dots.

The bosses everyone wants to work for stick with the script by connecting the dots. They make it clear to the people they lead and serve how they and their work matter.

## You Don't Know Jack—and Yes, You Should

There's a lot for you to think about and apply to your work. All I can do is make you aware of why, what, and how to flip your script, and stick with the flipped script, to maximize your chances for success as a new leader. You will never read a leadership book or attend a leadership course that will tell you, "If you do X, then Y will happen every single time with success," because we are human beings with feelings and emotions and imperfections—including the people who wrote those books or developed those courses.

But think about it. Being the boss everyone wants to work for does not mean you're always perfect. Rather, stick with your flipped script. Put the spotlight not on you, but on those you lead and serve. If you do that, they will feel like they and their work have meaning, which produces greater motivation, engagement, and better performance. They will believe they make a difference. Like Jack.

> *Jack has been with our company for 30 years. He started out as a mail courier, moved up to the Print Center, and now works in distribution. There, he makes sure the needs of leaders all over the world are fulfilled by packaging and shipping the publications and materials they need to become better leaders.*
>
> *In our service awards ceremony, Jack was able to give a speech to mark his 30 years. He acknowledged he'd never be a trainer and help participants. He knew he'd never be able to write a book to help leaders either. But if he didn't do his job, and those publications and materials never got out, those leaders would never get what they need to be great leaders. You see, Jack understands just how important his job is to our organization. Jack felt his work in the distribution center was just as important in helping leaders become the bosses everyone would want to work for as the work I personally do training them and writing this book.*

There are great lessons I have learned just by listening to Jack and his stories and seeing him at work. For instance, he knows exactly how his work matters, how important his job is to the organization, and how he makes a difference in the world. He connects the dots. No doubt, his leaders help him connect the dots as well, telling him just how important he is to them, their team, the organization, customers, clients—even the broader society. So should you with the people you lead and serve.

> *Jack also told me a story that happened long ago. The president of the organization at the time regularly walked the halls to visit every single department. The president was an old army guy, and this was his way of "visiting the troops." One day, the president asked Jack, working then as the mail courier, if he could ride along on his mail run.*
>
> *"The president wanted to ride along with me. Can you imagine that?" Jack said.*
>
> *During that ride, the president asked Jack's opinion on a company policy. Back then, the company usually gave bonuses to all workers at the end of the year, but the board had different ideas for how the money should be used that year.*
>
> *"Well, I told the president that the $100 or $200 we get as a year-end bonus might not sound like much to him or others high up in the company. But to people like me, that's a lot of money. We depend on it. We need it to survive. It makes us feel valued."*
>
> *The president went back to the board, and based on Jack's insight, everyone got that year-end bonus like they always did.*

To this day, Jack believes he made a difference that also helped his fellow employees, many of whom needed the money as much as he did. It was all because the president of the organization asked his opinion on how things were going and listened to what he had to say.

Now, there's no way we can please everybody, and sometimes decisions will go against popular opinion. But the president asking his opinion and listening to what he said made Jack feel so proud. Still does today. If an organization's president can do that for Jack, you can too for the people you lead and serve.

## You Can Flip Your Script and Stick With It Too

The ultimate flip for any leader, really, is feeling invested in the people you lead and serve more than feeling totally invested in your own success. And if you truly made the flip, you know that's exactly how you become successful and known as the boss everyone wants to work for. Ultimately as leaders, we are called to serve others, help others grow, and make the world around us a better place. Think about the greatest leaders of all time. Their greatest triumphs and achievements may not be attributed straight to them. And they truly believe that's the way it should be. They've clearly flipped their script.

You can too.

You have the capability and capacity to make others feel wanted, needed, and special at work. You have the power to make them feel valued and appreciated. You can outline exactly what they do and how it matters to you, your organization, and even society at large. That's a rare commodity in organizations right now, and it is sorely missed. You have the ability to flip your script and stick with it. Don't take it for granted.

While I hope this book truly has given you a model, a game plan, a blueprint to flip your script and stick with it, more than that, I hope this book gives you hope. You can make it as a new leader. Flip your script. You'll have more people who feel like Jack, engaged and proud of their work because you helped them feel that way.

As a new leader, you have the potential and ability to be the boss everyone wants to work for.

I believe you can do it. Now, go do it.

**THE COACH'S CORNER—YOU CAN STICK WITH YOUR FLIPPED SCRIPT**

If you are interested in digging deeper into ways to stick with your flipped script to be the boss everyone wants to work for, go to the companion website and find out more in the resources section for this chapter.

Here are two questions and two applications to help you stick with your flipped script.

**Question 1: What would happen if you and others flipped their script?** Imagine if all the managers in your organization flipped their scripts. How would you better serve your customers? How would people in your organization be happier and more engaged in their work? What would the culture of your organization look like?

**Question 2: How did the best boss you ever worked for connect your dots?** Think about the best boss you ever worked for. What did that person do to help you connect your dots, to help you feel appreciated, valued, or like you mattered? What can you learn from that person to help you do the same for the people you lead and serve?

**Application 1: Share "Jack" stories.** Sometime in the next 90 days, bring in a person whose life was directly touched by the work of your staff or team, and have this person share his or her story. Can't physically bring in a person? Share personal stories of gratitude of how helpful your staff or team was for customers or internal stakeholders. Sharing these stories reminds the people you lead and serve just how valued their work is, and will inspire others and reinforce how their work and lives matter.

**Application 2: Recognize achievements.** Find out one thing each of your direct reports, or staff or team members, has done that has met or exceeded your expectation of performance. In the next seven days, in person (or by phone if they aren't physically where you work), give these people SBI feedback on what they did, and thank all of them for their work and service.

# Taking the First Step

Flipping your script is hard. But you can do it. This book, the resources on the companion website, and your peers, colleagues, and boss (if you ask) are all there to help.

But to truly flip your script, take that first step. Here's how:

**Step 1: Select the one part of your script you want to flip.** You've read the book now. All parts are important, but what is the one part of your script you firmly believe will help you be the boss everyone wants to work for? And how can you get your own boss to support you in flipping your script in this one area?

**Step 2: Set a goal to flip your script; then share it, and get feedback.** It's not just knowing what part of your script you want to flip. Now, put it into action.

- Set a specific, difficult, yet attainable goal (like you read about in Chapter 5) that is linked to the most important part of your script you want to flip.

- Share what that goal is with others (for example, your boss, your direct reports, your team, staff, coworkers).
- Ask those people to give you feedback on how well you are progressing at attaining that goal over the next 66 days.[1]

**Step 3: Write a letter to your future self.**  You have learned a lot about being a leader in reading this book. Write a letter to yourself, detailing how you want to be the boss everyone wants to work for in the future and what you will do to flip your script and stick with it. Make sure to include in that letter the one goal you just made. Remember, use all the right mindchatter—be positive, optimistic, motivational, and use *you* and *your* in your letter. End on a positive note, confident of your future success.

Mail the letter to yourself, and open it 66 days from the day you receive it.

**Bonus:**  Want more support to flip your script? Tell people through Facebook or Instagram or LinkedIn. Hit me up on Twitter (@Lead_Better) and tell me (and the twittersphere) your goal, using #BeTheBossBook. Or, e-mail me your goal at William@WilliamGentryLeads.com.

If you truly want to flip your script, you can. You've got this.

# Notes

## INTRODUCTION

1. K. Lamoureaux and K. O'Leonard, *Leadership Development Factbook® 2009: Benchmarks and Analysis of Leadership Development Spending, Staffing and Programs*, Bersin & Associates (October 2009).

2. A. De Smet, M. McGurk, and M. Vinson, "How Companies Manage the Front Line Today: McKinsey Survey Results," McKinsey & Company (February 2010), http://www.mckinsey.com/insights/organization /how_companies_manage_the_front_line_today_mckinsey_survey _results.

3. Manchester International, "Why Are So Many Newly Promoted Managers & Executives Failing?" (2001), http://www.prnewswire.com /news-releases/manchester-consulting-why-are-so-many-newly-promoted -managers—executives-failing-77350667.html.

4. W. A. Gentry, "Derailment: How Successful Leaders Avoid It," in *The ASTD Leadership Handbook*, ed. E. Biech (Alexandria, VA: ASTD Press, 2010), 311–24; and W. A. Gentry and C. T. Chappelow, "Managerial Derailment: Weaknesses That Can Be Fixed," in *The Perils of Accentuating the Positives*, ed. R. B. Kaiser (Tulsa, OK: Hogan Press, 2009), 97–113.

5. P. Crush, "Cooper: Engagement Programmes Have Had No Impact on Wellbeing," *HR* (January 26, 2015), http://www.hrmagazine.co.uk /article-details/cooper-engagement-programmes-have-had-no-impact-on -wellbeing.

6. R. S. Wellins, A. Selkovits, and D. McGrath, *Be Better Than Average: A Study on the State of Frontline Leadership* (Bridgeville, PA: Development Dimensions International, 2013).

7. CareerBuilder Survey, "More Than One-Quarter of Managers Said They Weren't Ready to Lead When They Began Managing Others, Finds New CareerBuilder Survey" (March 28, 2011), http://www.careerbuilder .com/share/aboutus/pressreleasesdetail.aspx?id=pr626&sd=3%2F28% 2F2011&ed=12%2F31%2F2011.

8. A. De Smet, M. McGurk, and M. Vinson, "Unlocking the Potential of Frontline Managers," McKinsey & Company (August 2009), http:// www.mckinsey.com/business-functions/organization/our-insights/ unlocking-the-potential-of-frontline-managers.

9. K. O'Leonard and J. Krider, *Leadership Development Factbook® 2014: Benchmarks and Trends in U.S. Leadership Development*, BERSIN by Deloitte (May 2014).

10. K. O'Leonard and L. Loew, *Leadership Development Factbook® 2012: Benchmarks and Trends in U.S. Leadership Development*, Bersin & Associates Factbook Report (July 2012).

**CHAPTER 1**

1. R. E. Riggio, "Leaders: Born or Made?," *Psychology Today* (March 18, 2009), https://www.psychologytoday.com/blog/cutting-edge-leadership /200903/leaders-born-or-made; R. E. Riggio, "What Is Charisma and Charismatic Leadership?," *Psychology Today* (October 7, 2012), https://www .psychologytoday.com/blog/cutting-edge-leadership/201210/what-is-charisma -and-charismatic-leadership; and R. D. Arvey, M. Rotundo, W. Johnson, Z. Zhang, and M. McGue, "The Determinants of Leadership Role Occupancy: Genetic and Personality Factors," *Leadership Quarterly* 17, no. 1 (2006): 1–20.

2. W. A. Gentry, J. J. Deal, S. Stawiski, and M. Ruderman, *Are Leaders Born or Made? Perspectives from the Executive Suite*, White Paper (Greensboro, NC: Center for Creative Leadership, 2012), http://insights.ccl .org/wp-content/uploads/2015/02/AreLeadersBornOrMade.pdf.

3. B. Brown, "The Power of Vulnerability," Tedx Houston (June 2010), https://www.ted.com/talks/brene_brown_on_vulnerability?language=en.

4. B. Brown, *Daring Greatly: How the Courage to Be Vulnerable Transforms the Way We Live, Love, Parent, and Lead* (New York: Penguin/Gotham, 2012).

5. M. W. McCall, M. M. Lombardo, and A. W. Morrison, *The Lessons of Experience: How Successful Executives Develop on the Job* (Lexington, MA: Lexington Books, 1988); and J. Yip and M. Wilson, "Learning from Experience," in *Handbook of Leadership Development*, 3rd ed., ed. E. Van Velsor, C. D. McCauley, and M. N. Ruderman (San Francisco: Jossey Bass, 2010), 63–95.

**CHAPTER 2**

1. M. W. McCall Jr. and M. M. Lombardo, *Off the Track: Why and How Successful Executives Get Derailed* (Greensboro, NC: Center for Creative Leadership, 1983).

2. G. R. Ferris, R. Zinko, R. L. Brouer, M. R. Buckley, and M. G. Harvey, "Strategic Bullying as a Supplementary, Balanced Perspective on Destructive Leadership," *Leadership Quarterly* 18 (2007): 195–206; and M. Harvey, M. R. Buckley, J. T. Heames, R. Zinko, R. G. Brouer, and G. R. Ferris, "A Bully as an Archetypal Destructive Leader," *Journal of Leadership & Organizational Studies* 14 (2007): 117–29.

3. Gentry, "Derailment: How Successful Leaders Avoid It."

4. I wish to acknowledge and thank Professors Christopher Myers and Scott DeRue for their help and for allowing me to use their learning and motivation assessment for my research.

5. C. S. Dweck, *Mindset: The New Psychology of Success* (New York: Ballantine Books, 2008).

6. P. A. Heslin, G. P. Latham, and D. Vandewalle, "The Effect of Implicit Person Theory on Performance Appraisals," *Journal of Applied Psychology* 90 (2005): 842–56.

7. E. Van Velsor, C. D. McCauley, and M. Ruderman, eds., *The Center for Creative Leadership Handbook of Leadership Development*, 3rd ed. (San Francisco, CA: Jossey-Bass, 2010).

8. S. G. Rogelberg, L. Justice, P. W. Braddy, S. C. Paustian-Underdahl, E. Heggestad, L. Shanock, B. E. Baran, T. Beck, S. Long, A. Andrew, D. G. Altman, and J. W. Fleenor, "The Executive Mind: Leader Self-Talk, Effectiveness, and Strain," *Journal of Managerial Psychology* 28 (2012): 183–201.

9. Some of the ideas presented are based on information from these websites: C. Dweck, "How Can You Change from a Fixed Mindset to a Growth Mindset?," Mindset (n.d.), http://mindsetonline.com/changeyour

mindset/firststeps/; and T. Waghorn, "Are You Trapped in a Fixed Mindset? Fix It!," *Forbes* (April 20, 2009), http://www.forbes.com/2009/04/20 /mindset-psychology-succcess-leadership-careers-dweck.html.

## CHAPTER 3

1. A. Crippen, "Warren Buffett's $100,000 Offer and $500,000 Advice for Columbia Business School Students," CNBC (November 12, 2009), http://www.cnbc.com/id/33891448.

2. Paige Logan, a former student at Davidson College, and her professor Scott Tonidandel, both of whom were instrumental in examining these challenges. I'm indebted to them for their help.

3. R. L. Birdwhistell, *Kinesics and Context: Essays on Body Motion Communication* (Philadelphia: University of Pennsylvania Press, 1970).

4. A. Mehrabian, "Communication without Words," *Psychology Today* 2, no. 9 (1968): 52–55.

5. C. I. Brooks, M. A. Church, and L. Fraser, "Effects of Duration of Eye Contact on Judgments of Personality Characteristics," *Journal of Social Psychology* 126 (1986): 71–78; and D. Butler and F. L. Geis, "Nonverbal Affect Responses to Male and Female Leaders: Implications for Leadership Evaluations," *Journal of Personality and Social Psychology* 58 (1990): 48–59.

6. V. P. Richmond and J. C. McCroskey, *Nonverbal Behavior in Interpersonal Relations*, 4th ed. (Boston: Allyn and Bacon, 2000).

7. T. V. McGovern and H. E. Tinsley, "Interviewer Evaluations of Interviewee Nonverbal Behavior," *Journal of Vocational Behavior* 13 (1978): 163–71.

8. D. Desteno, C. Breazeal, R. H. Frank, D. Pizarro, J. Baumann, L. Dickens, and J. J. Lee, "Detecting the Trustworthiness of Novel Partners in Economic Exchange," *Psychological Science* 23 (2012): 1549–56.

9. S. Nowicki Jr. and M. P. Duke, *Helping the Child Who Doesn't Fit in* (Atlanta: Peachtree Publishers, 1992); and S. Nowicki Jr. and M. P. Duke, *Will I Ever Fit In? The Breakthrough Program for Conquering Adult Dyssemia* (New York: Free Press, 2002.)

10. W. A. Gentry and M. P. Duke, "A Historical Perspective on Nonverbal Communication in Debates: Implications for Elections and Leadership," *Journal of Leadership Studies* 2, no. 4 (2009): 36–47.

11. E. T. Hall, *The Silent Language* (Greenwich, CT: Fawcett, 1969).

12. A. Cuddy, "Your Body Language Shapes Who You Are," Ted Global (June 2012), https://www.ted.com/talks/amy_cuddy_your_body _language_shapes_who_you_are?language=en.

13. A. J. C. Cuddy, *Presence: Bringing Your Boldest Self to Your Biggest Challenges* (New York: Little, Brown, & Co., 2015).

14. R. E. Axtell, *Essential Do's and Taboos: The Complete Guide to International Business and Leisure Travel* (Hoboken, NJ: John Wiley & Sons, 2007); T. Morrison and W. A. Conaway, *Kiss, Bow, or Shake Hands: The Bestselling Guide to Doing Business in More Than 60 Countries* (Avon, MA: Adams Media, 2006); S. Ting-Toomey, *Communicating Across Cultures* (New York: Guilford Press, 1999); and D. W. Prince and M. H. Hoppe, *Communicating Across Cultures* (Greensboro, NC: CCL Press, 2000).

15. Nowicki Jr. and Duke, *Helping the Child Who Doesn't Fit In*; and Gentry and Duke, "A Historical Perspective on Nonverbal Communication in Debates."

16. D. L. Joseph, L. Y. Dhanani, W. Shen, B. C. McHugh, and M. A. McCord, "Is a Happy Leader a Good Leader? A Meta-Analytic Investigation of Leader Trait Affect and Leadership," *Leadership Quarterly* 26 (2015): 557–76.

17. R. Rajah, Z. Song, and R. D. Arvey, "Emotionality and Leadership: Taking Stock of the Past Decade of Research," *Leadership Quarterly* 22 (2011): 1107–19.

18. V. A. Visser, D. van Knippenberg, G. A. van Kleef, and B. Wisse, "How Leader Displays of Happiness and Sadness Influence Follower Performance: Emotional Contagion and Creative versus Analytical Performance," *Leadership Quarterly* 24 (2013): 172–88.

19. J. H. K. Wong and E. K. Kelloway, "What Happens at Work Stays at Work? Workplace Supervisory Social Interactions and Blood Pressure Outcomes," *Journal of Occupational Health Psychology* 21 (2016): 133–41; M. Oaklander, "How Your Boss Can Raise Your Blood Pressure," *Time* (December 15, 2015), http://time.com/4148617/blood-pressure-boss -stress/.

20. G. Sadri, T. J. Weber, and W. A. Gentry, "Empathic Emotion and Leadership Performance: An Empirical Analysis across 38 Countries," *Leadership Quarterly* 22 (2011): 818–30.

21. W. A. Gentry, M. A. Clark, S. F. Young, K. L. Cullen, and L. Zimmerman, "How Displaying Empathic Concern May Differentially Predict Career Derailment Potential for Women and Men Leaders in Australia," *Leadership Quarterly* 26 (2015): 641–53.

22. K. E. Brink and R. D. Costigan, "Oral Communication Skills: Are the Priorities of the Workplace and AACSB-Accredited Business Programs Aligned?," *Academy of Management Learning & Education* 14 (2015): 205–21.

23. C. A. Higgins, T. A. Judge, and G. R. Ferris, "Influence Tactics and Work Outcomes: A Meta-Analysis," *Journal of Organizational Behavior* 24 (2003): 89–106.

24. G. Yukl, "Influence tactics for leaders," in *The ASTD Leadership Handbook*, ed. E. Biech (Alexandria, VA: ASTD Press, 2010), 73–87; and G. Yukl, C. Seifert, and C. Chavez, "Validation of the Extended Influence Behavior Questionnaire," *Leadership Quarterly* 19 (2008): 609–21.

## CHAPTER 4

1. "I Have a Best Friend at Work," *Gallup Business Journal* (May 26, 1999), http://www.gallup.com/businessjournal/511/item-10-best-friend -work.aspx.

2. K. A. Jehn and P. P. Shah, "Interpersonal Relationships and Task Performance: An Examination of Mediation Processes in Friendship and Acquaintance Groups," *Journal of Personality and Social Psychology* 72 (1997): 775–90.

3. C. M. Riordan and R. W. Griffeth, "The Opportunity for Friendship in the Workplace: An Underexplored Construct," *Journal of Business and Psychology* 10 (1995): 141–54.

4. C. R. Gerstner and D. V. Day, "Meta-Analytic Review of Leader-Member Exchange Theory: Correlates and Construct Issues," *Journal of Applied Psychology* 82 (1997): 827–44.

5. D. J. Henderson, S. J. Wayne, L. M. Shore, W. H. Bommer, and L. E. Tetrick, "Leader-Member Exchange, Differentiation, and Psychological Contract Fulfillment: A Multilevel Examination," *Journal of Applied Psychology* 93 (2008): 1208–19.

6. T. A. Judge, R. F. Piccolo, and R. Ilies, "The Forgotten Ones? A Re-Examination of Consideration, Initiating Structure, and Leadership Effectiveness," *Journal of Applied Psychology* 89 (2004): 36–51.

7. Gentry, "Derailment: How Successful Leaders Avoid It."

8. C. S. Burke, K. C. Stagl, C. Klein, G. F. Goodwin, E. Salas, and S. M. Halpin, "What Type of Leadership Behaviors Are Functional in Teams? A Meta-Analysis," *Leadership Quarterly* 17 (2006): 288–307.

9. W. H. Drath, C. D. McCauley, C. J. Palus, E. Van Velsor, P. M. G. O'Connor, and J. B. McGuire, "Direction, Alignment, Commitment: Toward a More Integrative Ontology of Leadership," *Leadership Quarterly* 19 (2008): 635–53; and C. McCauley, *Making Leadership Happen*, White Paper (Greensboro, NC: Center for Creative Leadership, 2014), http://insights.ccl.org/wp-content/uploads/2015/04/MakingLeadershipHappen.pdf.

10. J. Rozovsky, "The Five Keys to a Successful Google Team," *re:Work, The Water Cooler* (November 17, 2015), https://rework.withgoogle.com/blog/five-keys-to-a-successful-google-team/.

11. A. C. Edmondson and Z. Lei, "Psychological Safety: The History, Renaissance, and Future of an Interpersonal Construct," *Annual Review of Organizational Psychology and Organizational Behavior* 1 (2014): 23–43.

12. E. L. Deci and R. M. Ryan, *Intrinsic Motivation and Self-Determination in Human Behavior* (New York: Plenum, 1985); and E. L. Deci and R. M. Ryan, *Handbook of Self-Determination Research* (Rochester, NY: University of Rochester Press, 2002).

13. C. Heath, "On the Social Psychology of Agency Relationships: Lay Theories of Motivation Overemphasize Extrinsic Incentives," *Organizational Behavior and Human Decision Processes* 78 (1999): 25–62.

14. G. D. Jenkins, A. Mitra, N. Gupta, and J. D. Shaw, "Are Financial Incentives Related to Performance? A Meta-Analytic Review of Empirical Research," *Journal of Applied Psychology* 83 (1998): 777–87.

15. D. H. Pink, *Drive: The Surprising Truth about What Motivates Us* (New York: Riverhead Books, 2011).

16. Y. J. Cho and J. L. Perry, "Intrinsic Motivation and Employee Attitudes: Role of Managerial Trustworthiness, Goal Directedness, and Extrinsic Reward Expectancy," *Review of Public Personnel Administration* 32 (2012): 382–406.

17. K. Woolley and A. Fishbach, "The Experience Matters More Than You Think: People Value Intrinsic Incentives More Inside Than Outside an Activity," *Journal of Personality and Social Psychology* 109 (2015): 968–82.

18. J. Pfeffer, "Six Dangerous Myths about Pay," *Harvard Business Review* 76, no. 3 (1998): 109–19.

19. L. M. Graves, K. L. Cullen, H. F. Lester, M. N. Ruderman, and W. A. Gentry, "Managerial Motivational Profiles: Composition, Antecedents, and Consequences," *Journal of Vocational Behavior* 87 (2015): 32–42.

## CHAPTER 5

1. S. W. J. Kozlowski, S. M. Gully, E. Salas, and J. A. Cannon-Bowers, "Team Leadership and Development: Theory, Principles, and Guidelines for Training Leaders and Teams," in *Advances in Interdisciplinary Studies of Work Teams: Team Leadership*, Vol. 3, ed. M. Beyerlein, D. Johnson, and S. Beyerlein (Greenwich, CT: JAI Press, 1996), 251–89.

2. S. Lauby, "Interview: Dr. Eduardo Salas on Best Practices for Developing Teamwork," HR Bartender (August 18, 2013), https://www.hrbartender.com/2013/training/interview-dr-eduardo-salas-on-best-practices-for-developing-teamwork/.

3. T. D. Allen, L. T. Eby, M. L. Poteet, E. Lentz, and L. Lima, "Career Benefits Associated with Mentoring for Protégés: A Meta-Analysis," *Journal of Applied Psychology* 89 (2004): 127–36.

4. A. Ramaswami and G. F. Dreher, "The Benefits Associated with Workplace Mentoring Relationships," in *Blackwell Handbook of Mentoring: A Multiple Perspectives Approach*, ed. T. D. Allen and L. T. Eby (London: Blackwell, 2007), 211–31.

5. R. Ghosh and T. G. Reio Jr., "Career Benefits Associated with Mentoring for Mentors: A Meta-Analysis," *Journal of Vocational Behavior* 83 (2013): 106–16.

6. W. A. Gentry, T. J. Weber, and G. Sadri, "Examining Career-Related Mentoring and Managerial Performance across Cultures: A Multilevel Analysis," *Journal of Vocational Behavior* 72 (2008): 241–53.

7. W. A. Gentry and J. J. Sosik, "Developmental Relationships and Managerial Promotability in Organizations: A Multisource Study," *Journal of Vocational Behavior* 77 (2010): 266–78.

8. W. A. Gentry, "Mentoring for Leadership Development," in *The Center for Creative Leadership Handbook of Coaching in Organizations*, ed. D. D. Riddle, E. R. Hoole, and E. C. D. Gullette (San Francisco: Jossey-Bass, 2015), 247–82.

9. K. E. Kram, *Mentoring at Work* (Glenview, IL: Scott, Foresman, 1985).

10. G. P. Latham and E. A. Locke, "Goal Setting—A Motivational Technique That Works," *Organizational Dynamics* 8, no. 2 (1979): 68–80; E. A. Locke and G. P. Latham, *Goal-Setting: A Motivational Technique That Works* (Englewood Cliffs, NJ: Prentice-Hall, 1984); and E. A. Locke, K. N. Shaw, L. M. Saari, and G. P. Latham, "Goal Setting and Task Performance: 1969–1980," *Psychological Bulletin* 90 (1981): 125–52.

11. D. S. Yeager, V. Purdie-Vaughns, J. Garcia, N. Apfel, P. Brzustoski, A. Master, W. T. Hessert, M. E. Williams, and G. L. Cohen, "Breaking the Cycle of Mistrust: Wise Interventions to Provide Critical Feedback across the Racial Divide," *Journal of Experimental Psychology: General* 143, no. 2 (2014): 804–24.

12. P. E. Levy and J. R. Williams, "The Social Context of Performance Appraisal: A Review and Framework for the Future," *Journal of Management* 30 (2004): 881–905.

13. J. M. Gottman, *What Predicts Divorce?* (Hillsdale, NJ: Lawrence Erlbaum Associates, 1994).

## CHAPTER 6

1. G. R. Ferris and W. A. Hochwarter, "Organizational Politics," in *APA Handbook of Industrial and Organizational Psychology*, Vol. 3, ed. S. Zedeck (Washington, DC: American Psychological Association, 2011), 435–59; G. R. Ferris, D. C. Treadway, R. L. Brouer, and T. P. Munyon, "Political Skill in the Organizational Sciences," in *Politics in Organizations: Theory and Research Considerations*, ed. G. R. Ferris and D. C. Treadway (New York: Routledge/Taylor and Francis, 2012), 487–549; G. R. Ferris, D. C. Treadway, R. W. Kolodinsky, W. A. Hochwarter, C. J. Kacmar, C. Douglas, and D. D. Frink, "Development and Validation of the Political Skill Inventory," *Journal of Management* 31 (2005): 126–52; and G. R. Ferris, D. C. Treadway, P. L. Perrewé, R. L. Brouer, C. Douglas, and S. Lux, "Political Skill in Organizations," *Journal of Management* 33 (2007): 290–320.

2. P. L. Perrewé, C. C. Rosen, and C. Maslach, "Organizational Politics and Stress: The Development of a Process Model," in *Politics in Organizations: Theory and Research Considerations*, ed. G. R. Ferris and D. C. Treadway (New York: Taylor & Francis, 2012), 213–55.

3. W. A. Gentry, R. Eckert, V. P. Munusamy, S. A. Stawiski, and J. Martin, "The Needs of Participants in Leadership Development Programs: A Qualitative and Quantitative, Cross-Country Investigation," *Journal of Leadership & Organizational Studies* 21 (2014): 83–101.

4. G. R. Ferris, S. L. Davidson, and P. L. Perrewé, *Political Skill at Work: Impact on Work Effectiveness* (Mountain View, CA: Davies-Black, 2005).

5. W. A. Gentry and J. B. Leslie, *Developing Political Savvy* (Greensboro, NC: CCL Press, 2012).

6. T. P. Munyon, J. K. Summers, K. M. Thompson, and G. R. Ferris, "Political Skill and Work Outcomes: A Theoretical Extension, Meta-Analytic Investigation, and Agenda for the Future," *Personnel Psychology* 68 (2015): 143–84.

7. W. A. Gentry, D. C. Gilmore, M. L. Shuffler, and J. B. Leslie, "Political Skill as an Indicator of Promotability among Multiple Rater Sources," *Journal of Organizational Behavior* 33 (2012): 89–104; and W. A. Gentry, J. B. Leslie, D. C. Gilmore, B. P. Ellen III, G. R. Ferris, and D. C. Treadway, "Personality and Political Skill as Distal and Proximal Predictors of Leadership Evaluations," *Career Development International* 18 (2013): 569–88.

8. J. B. Leslie and W. A. Gentry, *Women and Political Savvy: How to Build and Embrace a Fundamental Leadership Skill*, White Paper (Greensboro, NC: Center for Creative Leadership, 2012), http://insights.ccl.org /wp-content/uploads/2015/04/WomenPoliticalSavvy.pdf.

9. P. Wilburn and K. Cullen, *A Leader's Network: How to Help Your Talent Invest in the Right Relationships at the Right Time*, White Paper (Greensboro, NC: Center for Creative Leadership, 2014), http://insights.ccl .org/wp-content/uploads/2015/04/LeadersNetwork.pdf.

10. A. Grant, "5 Myths about Introverts and Extroverts at Work," Huff Post, The Third Metric (February 19, 2014; updated April 21, 2014), http://www.huffingtonpost.com/adam-grant/5-myths-about-introverts_b _4814390.html.

**CHAPTER 7**

1. A. Berenson, "The Tyco Mistrial: The Chief; Tyco Chief and His Deputy Avoid Convictions, but Not Tattered Reputations," *New York Times*, Business Day (April 3, 2004), http://www.nytimes.com/2004/04

/03/business/tyco-mistrial-chief-tyco-chief-his-deputy-avoid-convictions -but-not-tattered.html?_r=0.

2. J. J. Sosik, W. A. Gentry, and J. U. Chun, "The Value of Virtue in the Upper Echelons: A Multisource Examination of Executive Character Strengths and Performance," *Leadership Quarterly* 23 (2012): 367–82; and W. A. Gentry, K. L. Cullen, J. J. Sosik, J. U. Chun, C. R. Leupold, and S. Tonidandel, "Integrity's Place among the Character Strengths of Middle-Level Managers and Top-Level Executives," *Leadership Quarterly* 24 (2013): 395–404.

3. C. Peterson and M. E. P. Seligman, *Character Strengths and Virtues: A Handbook and Classification* (New York: Oxford/American Psychological Association, 2004).

4. "Measuring the Return on Character," *Harvard Business Review* (April 2015), https://hbr.org/2015/04/measuring-the-return-on -character.

5. "Interview with Ken Lay," CNN.com, *Larry King Live* (July 12, 2004), http://www.cnn.com/TRANSCRIPTS/0407/12/lkl.00.html.

6. W. A. Gentry, K. L. Cullen, and D. G. Altman, *The Irony of Integrity: A Study of the Character Strengths of Leaders*, White Paper (Greensboro, NC: Center for Creative Leadership, 2012), http://insights.ccl .org/wp-content/uploads/2015/04/IronyOfIntegrity.pdf.

7. C. Joffe-Walt and A. Spigel, "Psychology of Fraud: Why Good People Do Bad Things," NPR, *All Things Considered* (May 1, 2012), http://www.npr.org/2012/05/01/151764534/psychology-of-fraud-why-good -people-do-bad-things.

8. M. H. Bazerman and A. E. Tenbrunsel, *Blind Spots: Why You Don't Do What's Right and What to Do about It* (Princeton, NJ: Princeton University Press, 2011).

9. N. Nohria, "You're Not as Virtuous as You Think," *Washington Post* (October 15, 2015), https://www.washingtonpost.com/opinions/youre-not -as-virtuous-as-you-think/2015/10/15/fec227c4-66b4-11e5-9ef3 -fde182507eac_story.html.

10. R. C. Mayer, J. H. Davis, and F. D. Schoorman, "An Integrative Model of Organizational Trust," *Academy of Management Review* 20 (1995): 709–34.

11. J. A. Colquitt, B. A. Scott, and J. A. LePine, "Trust, Trustworthi- ness, and Trust Propensity: A Meta-Analytic Test of Their Unique

Relationships with Risk Taking and Job Performance," *Journal of Applied Psychology* 92 (2007): 909–27.

12. McCall, Lombardo, and Morrison, *The Lessons of Experience.*

**CHAPTER 8**

1. R. Eisenberger, R. Huntington, S. Hutchison, and D. Sowa, "Perceived Organizational Support," *Journal of Applied Psychology* 71 (1986): 500–507.

2. J. N. Kurtessis, R. Eisenberger, M. T. Ford, L. C. Buffardi, K. A. Stewart, and C. S. Adis, "Perceived Organizational Support: A Meta-Analytic Evaluation of Organizational Support Theory," *Journal of Management* (in press).

3. R. Eisenberger, F. Stinglhamber, C. Vandenberghe, I. L. Sucharski, and L. Rhoades, "Perceived Supervisor Support: Contributions to Perceived Organizational Support and Employee Retention," *Journal of Applied Psychology* 87 (2002): 565–73.

4. A. M. Grant, *Give and Take: A Revolutionary Approach to Success* (New York: Viking Press, 2013).

5. A. M. Grant, "Relational Job Design and the Motivation to Make a Prosocial Difference," *Academy of Management Review* 32 (2007): 393–417; A. M. Grant, "The Significance of Task Significance: Job Performance Effects, Relational Mechanisms, and Boundary Conditions," *Journal of Applied Psychology* 93 (2008): 108–24; and A. M. Grant and S. Sonnentag, "Doing Good Buffers against Feeling Bad: Prosocial Impact Compensates for Negative Task and Self-Evaluations," *Organizational Behavior and Human Decision Processes* 111 (2010): 13–22.

6. A. M. Grant, "Leading with Meaning: Beneficiary Contact, Prosocial Impact, and the Performance Effects of Transformational Leadership," *Academy of Management Journal* 55 (2012): 458–76; A. M. Grant, "How Customers Can Rally Your Troops: End Users Can Energize Your Workforce Far Better Than Your Managers Can," *Harvard Business Review* 89, no. 6 (June 2011): 97–103; and A. M. Grant, E. M. Campbell, G. Chen, K. Cottone, D. Lapedis, and K. Lee, "Impact and the Art of Motivation Maintenance: The Effects of Contact with Beneficiaries on Persistence Behavior," *Organizational Behavior and Human Decision Processes* 103 (2007): 53–67.

**TAKING THE FIRST STEP**

1. Why 66 days? Research by Phillippa Lally and colleagues found the most likely amount of time it took to form behaviors into a habit and accomplish their goal was 66 days. See M. Popova, "How Long It Takes to Form a New Habit," Brainpickings (January 2, 2014), http://www .brainpickings.org/2014/01/02/how-long-it-takes-to-form-a-new-habit/; and P. Lally, C. H. M. van Jaarsveld, J. W. W. Potts, and J. Wardle, "How Are Habits Formed: Modeling Habit Formation in the Real World," *European Journal of Social Psychology* 40 (2010): 998–1009.

# About the Research

Data for this book came from 297 first-time managers who attended the Center for Creative Leadership's Maximizing Your Leadership Potential program between May 2012 and December 2013. They averaged 36.57 years of age (SD = 7.82) and were majority men (55.2 percent). Leaders were from all over the world (65.7 percent from the United States), and well-educated (82.9 percent had a least a college education). Most (78.1 percent) worked in the private sector from several diverse industries (e.g., computer software and services; consumer products; energy; food, beverage, tobacco; insurance; manufacturing; and pharmaceuticals). Qualitative data and quotes were slightly changed when there was identifying information, and fictitious names were used to protect the anonymity and confidentiality of these leaders.

# Acknowledgments

Many people have helped me make this book a reality. Some will be anonymous and some I'll name here, but all are special.

I want to thank all my Center for Creative Leadership colleagues. John Ryan, CCL President, thank you for believing in me and encouraging me to help leaders with this book. Kim Leahy, Katherine Pappa, David Horth, and Rachael Foy, thank you for giving me the idea years ago to do this book. Thank you Judy Turpin for entering my research data, and Braxton Walker for providing access to the data. I appreciate Karen Oboth for all of her work with the Maximizing Your Leadership Potential program, Maggie Sass for her continued support of my research with the program, and all the program coordinators I've worked with who make the experience easy for us trainers and special for our participants. The entire RIPD department has supported me along the way. Of those, I especially want to thank Jennifer Martineau, Emily Hoole, Jean Leslie, Tracy Patterson, and Marian Ruderman. For helping me get my work out there into places

I myself could not, thank you Portia Mount, Stephen Martin, Tina Miller, Tracy Dobbins, and Kelly Lombardino. And to John Stallings, I appreciate the last-minute help of reading the next-to-last version.

I was very lucky to have several interns help me with this book. Lauren Zimmerman, Meaghan Gartner, Ben Tarshish, Evan Skloot, Scott Weinreb, and Samuel Leslie, your futures are bright and I can't wait to see your careers flourish! Remember me when you make it to the top of your field.

To the Berrett-Koehler staff: you all are outstanding, everything an author would want from a publisher. A tremendous amount of gratitude goes especially to Neal Maillet for all of his editorial responsibilities and Jeevan Sivasubramaniam for keeping things moving. I also want to thank the three reviewers whose insight made this book even better.

To all my classmates, friends, teachers, and mentors, from McCallie, Emory, and UGA, thanks for your love and encouragement.

To my mom, thank you for all your support and believing in me. Dad, I know, is looking down, beaming with pride.

I especially want to call out two CCL colleagues who have been instrumental in making this book a reality. First, Pete Scisco: you represented me and my interests from the beginning, particularly with my Berrett-Koehler colleagues. You also read every single word, many times, and helped make my dream to be an author come true.

Second, my wife, Courtney: I thank God every day that He sent you to CCL and led us to find each other. You heard my frustrations, stood by me when I was at my worst and helpless, and celebrated every piece of good news and each milestone accomplished. You read every single word, came up with the title, told me when I wasn't hitting the mark, helped me say things better, and kept me striving to help all these new leaders and frontline managers out there. You've helped me be a better boss too. My partner in everything, my thanks, and my heart, to you.

# Index

# About the Author

**William A. (Bill) Gentry, PhD,** is currently the Director of Leadership Insights and Analytics and a Senior Research Scientist at the Center for Creative Leadership (CCL). He is also an adjunct assistant professor in the Psychology Department at Guilford College; an associate member of the graduate faculty in the Organizational Sciences doctoral program at the University of North Carolina, Charlotte; and has taught at several other colleges and universities.

Bill's research has been featured in more than 50 Internet and news outlets; he has more than 70 academic presentations and has published more than 40 peer-reviewed articles in such journals as the *Journal of Applied Psychology, Journal of Organizational Behavior, Journal of Vocational Behavior, Personnel Psychology, Personality and Social Psychology Bulletin,* and *The Leadership Quarterly.* He also serves on the editorial review boards of the *Journal of Business and Psychology, Journal of Organizational Behavior,* and *The Leadership Quarterly.* Aside from his research, Bill trains CCL's Assessment Certification

Workshop and Maximizing Your Leadership Potential programs.

Bill graduated summa cum laude from Emory University in 2000 and received his MS in 2002 and his PhD in 2005 in industrial-organizational psychology from the University of Georgia. In 2011, Bill was inducted into the inaugural class of the University of Georgia's 40 under 40, as one of the top 40 graduates of the University of Georgia under the age of 40.

You can follow Bill on Twitter: @Lead_Better. Visit his website, www.WilliamGentryLeads.com.

Center for
Creative
Leadership®

THE CENTER FOR CREATIVE LEADERSHIP (CCL®) is a top-ranked global provider of leadership development. By leveraging the power of leadership to drive results that matter most to clients, CCL transforms individual leaders, teams, organizations, and society. Its array of cutting-edge solutions is steeped in extensive research and experience gained from working with hundreds of thousands of leaders at all levels. Ranked among the world's top five providers of executive education by the *Financial Times* and in the Top 10 by *Bloomberg BusinessWeek*, CCL has offices in Greensboro, NC; Colorado Springs, CO; San Diego, CA; Brussels, Belgium; Moscow, Russia; Addis Ababa, Ethiopia; Johannesburg, South Africa; Singapore; Gurgaon, India; and Shanghai, China.

# About the Maximizing Your Leadership Potential Program

First-time and frontline managers don't have it easy.

Making the shift from successful individual contributor to effective manager can be tricky—and getting the best performance out of others is an ongoing challenge.

First-level managers and supervisors are working through key leadership challenges, in their day-to-day work. They seek better ways to:

- **Lead a team**—being "in charge" is different from being a contributor.
- **Get the work done**—new skills are needed to get results through others.
- **Deal with conflict**—interpersonal issues and disagreements can jeopardize teams, departments, and projects.
- **Solve problems**—bigger, more complicated issues are part of the job.

Maximizing Your Leadership Potential addresses your specific leadership challenges and prepares you to achieve results by leading others.

## Berrett–Koehler
Publishers

**Berrett-Koehler** is an independent publisher dedicated to an ambitious mission: *Connecting people and ideas to create a world that works for all.*

We believe that the solutions to the world's problems will come from all of us, working at all levels: in our organizations, in our society, and in our own lives. Our BK Business books help people make their organizations more humane, democratic, diverse, and effective (we don't think there's any contradiction there). Our BK Currents books offer pathways to creating a more just, equitable, and sustainable society. Our BK Life books help people create positive change in their lives and align their personal practices with their aspirations for a better world.

All of our books are designed to bring people seeking positive change together around the ideas that empower them to see and shape the world in a new way.

And we strive to practice what we preach. At the core of our approach is Stewardship, a deep sense of responsibility to administer the company for the benefit of all of our stakeholder groups including authors, customers, employees, investors, service providers, and the communities and environment around us. Everything we do is built around this and our other key values of quality, partnership, inclusion, and sustainability.

This is why we are both a B-Corporation and a California Benefit Corporation—a certification and a for-profit legal status that require us to adhere to the highest standards for corporate, social, and environmental performance.

We are grateful to our readers, authors, and other friends of the company who consider themselves to be part of the BK Community. We hope that you, too, will join us in our mission.

### A BK Business Book

We hope you enjoy this BK Business book. BK Business books pioneer new leadership and management practices and socially responsible approaches to business. They are designed to provide you with groundbreaking and practical tools to transform your work and organizations while upholding the triple bottom line of people, planet, and profits. High-five!

To find out more, visit **www.bkconnection.com**.

**Berrett–Koehler**
**BK** Publishers

Connecting people and ideas
to create a world that works for all

Dear Reader,

Thank you for picking up this book and joining our worldwide community of Berrett-Koehler readers. We share ideas that bring positive change into people's lives, organizations, and society.

**To welcome you, we'd like to offer you a free e-book.** You can pick from among twelve of our bestselling books by entering the promotional code **BKP92E** here: http://www.bkconnection.com/welcome.

When you claim your free e-book, we'll also send you a copy of our e-newsletter, the *BK Communiqué*. Although you're free to unsubscribe, there are many benefits to sticking around. In every issue of our newsletter you'll find

- A free e-book
- Tips from famous authors
- Discounts on spotlight titles
- Hilarious insider publishing news
- A chance to win a prize for answering a riddle

Best of all, our readers tell us, "Your newsletter is the only one I actually read." So claim your gift today, and please stay in touch!

Sincerely,

Charlotte Ashlock
Steward of the BK Website

Questions? Comments? Contact me at bkcommunity@bkpub.com.

MIX
Paper from
responsible sources
FSC
www.fsc.org   FSC® C002589

Certified
B
Corporation
bcorporation.net